Stands and Product Displays

Edition 2007

Author: Jacobo Krauel
Publisher: Carles Broto
Graphic design & production: Dimitris Kottas
Text: contributed by the architects, edited by Carme Márquez and William George

© Carles Broto i Comerma
Jonqueres, 10, 1-5
08003 Barcelona, Spain
Tel.: +34 93 301 21 99
 Fax: +34-93-301 00 21
E-mail: info@linksbooks.net
www. linksbooks.net

Stands and Product Displays

Index

Introduction

In today's media-saturated and design-savvy marketplace, a company's image is just as important to its success as the quality of the product or service it provides. Top companies dedicate a considerable part of their resources to creating a strong corporate image that sets them apart from competitors. Increasingly, this includes developing a strong presence at industry trade fairs, which play an important role in attracting potential clients. This situation has led many companies to engage the services of some of the leading names in architecture and design when planning their stands, and to the birth of a new hybrid discipline combining cutting-edge elements of both marketing and spatial design.

Designing a stand is a new kind of challenge for architects and designers. It requires them to transmit the essence of a company in a much smaller scale and time frame than traditional architecture, allowing them to experiment and propose unusual and innovative solutions. In order to be successful, a stand must balance a striking and eye-catching design with perfectly reflecting the company's products and image. The nearly 40 stands in this collection have been selected according to this criteria. Some of the most innovative architectural work being done today is illustrated here, with designers using unusual materials and the latest technology to differentiate their designs and create a lasting impression in a short time.

Ranging from modest one-room stalls to sprawling, multi-story stands and representing industries as diverse as jewelry, automobiles, construction materials and furniture, this collection surveys the spectrum of stand styles, from the simple and classy to high-tech or experimental designs. It includes the work of some of the most respected and brilliant professionals and design groups, such as Kauffmann Theilig & Partner, Quinze & Milan, Think Kubik., Zeeh Bahls and Michael Young. We hope this overview of the most interesting work being done in this rapidly evolving field will be a source of insight and inspiration for the reader.

Fairnet

Fairnet

Every year the 'Who's Who' of commerce meet at the EuroShop Fair in Düsseldorf, with 1,500 exhibitors and around 95,000 visitors, the world's biggest trade fair for the investment needs of traders. To sell the secrets of good trade and display communication, you have to play by those same rules. Fairnet's new marketing strategy is an example.

Fairnet was aware that potential clients failed to recognize the company's major asset, integrated solutions from a single source. The complexity of Fairnet's background network meant many clients had a vague image of what Fairnet really was.

Martin Buhl-Wagner, Fairnet's representative, explains the steps they followed to develop the brand strategically: "Fairnet needed a friendly and recognizable key image associated with positive emotions; an image combining all of Fairnet's assets but not existing previously in this industrial sector, thereby differentiating Fairnet from its competitors. The corporate design was revised. The color green remained central to Fairnet but was complemented with silver – the color of jewelry– and some secondary colors.

The creative strategy was based on emotional key images with a 'human touch', to represent the brand's promise to its clients, that everything will work smoothly, irrespective of how many of Fairnet's services are used.

The new slogan 'I run Fairnet' got the management and the employees exited."

Interaction with clients at fairs and exhibitions is vital to integrated communication. At EuroShop, Fairnet adapted a previously successful presentation to their new communication line. Based on the same 'foundations' – a terrace-like structure consisting of three platforms on different levels – a completely different structure was built. The shell consists of a series of square aluminum frames revolving around a fictitious central axis of adjustable height, covered by a translucent, web-like membrane.

In addition to the long information and drinks bar, which has already stood the test of time, small apples made of marzipan are served at another bar. Visitors can watch screen presentations at terminals or the film on Fairnet's range of services, their network and their references. The other slogan "Success comes when everything fits" expresses Fairnet's way into a future of integrated trade fair and display communication strategies, a challenge to the enterprise and an inspiration to their competitors.

DESIGN & CLIENT:
Fairnet
LOCATION:
EuroShop 2005, Dusseldorf, Germany
PHOTOGRAPHS:
Contributed by Fairnet

Ignasi Bonjoch

Sacresa 2006

The stand designed for Sacresa, the leading real estate company, occupied a surface area on the ground floor of 264 sqm, plus 110 sqm more on the floor above, totaling 374 sqm of usable space, located at one end of the trade show building. This provided an almost blank rear wall with slit openings, while the other three walls remained open to the public. The brief was clearly defined: to occupy the ground floor with the attendance area for the general public, with the scale models of the buildings under promotion, plus a service space with a storage room and a kitchen. The floor above had a meeting room able to accommodate 10 persons with their audiovisual equipment, and a conversation lounge with several different areas.

The whole construction consisted of a steel structural frame of support members and beams, totally clad in reusable timber. A white T-shaped volume rested on a series of bridges over the steel structure. Its fully glazed side were a perfect viewpoint over the whole trade show. The ceiling consisted of closely spaced wooden beams that concealed the lighting fixtures; a black, sprinkler-compatible fabric enclosed the space from above.

To orchestrate visual access between the two floors, designer Ignasi Bonjoch laid a network of swiveling aluminum slats over the steel supporting structure, thereby projecting a pattern of light and shadow onto the black carpet of the floor below, like a sun screen. Little spotlights were placed between the slats, to illuminate the scale models, displayed on mirror-clad plinths.

The longitudinal disposition of the ground floor was only broken by three transversal lines, that formed a narrow path or aisle across the space. The aisle's mirror clad walls displayed a selection of photographs of Sacresa's most significant buildings. The reflections and counterreflections created a feeling of infinity, enveloping the visitors in a multiplicity of images, underlined by the red floor-carpet in this area.

CLIENT:
Sacresa
LOCATION:
SIMA Madrid 2006, Ifema Madrid
ARCHITECTURE:
Ignasi Bonjoch
COLLABORATORS:
Guillem Hortoneda,
Cristian Marín, (designers)
DATE:
April 2006
SURFACE:
2900 sqft (280 sqmt)
COST:
125.000 €
PHOTOGRAPHS:
Miguel de Guzmán

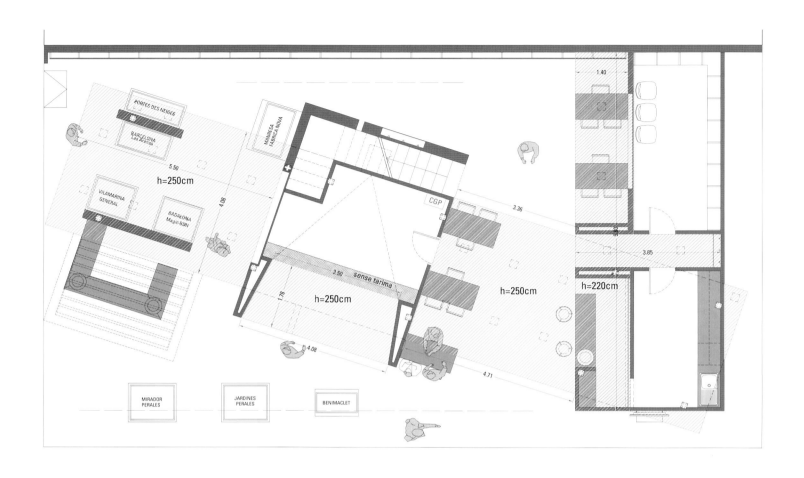

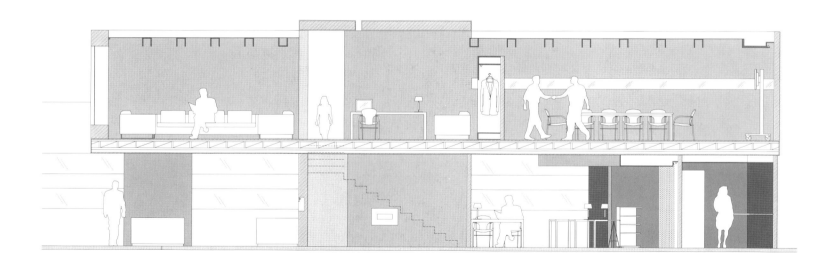

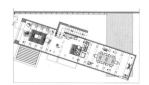

16

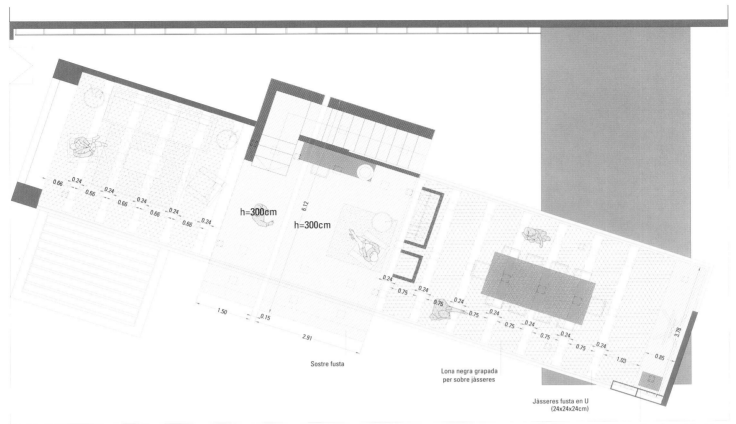

0.66 0.24
  0.66   0.24
      0.66   0.24
          0.66   0.24
              0.66   0.24

h=300cm

h=300cm

6.12

0.24
  0.75   0.24
      0.75   0.24
          0.75   0.24
              0.75   0.24
                  0.75   0.24
                      0.75   0.24
                          1.03   0.85

3.78

1.50   0.15

2.91

Sostre fusta

Lona negra grapada
per sobre jàsseres

Jàsseres fusta en U
(24x24x24cm)

Sostre fusta amb fossejat
per fluorescència

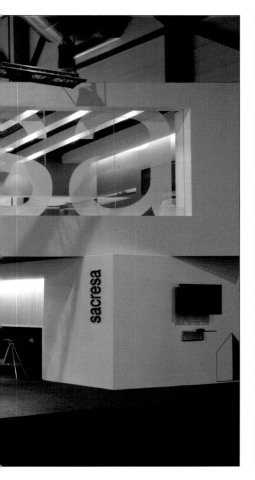

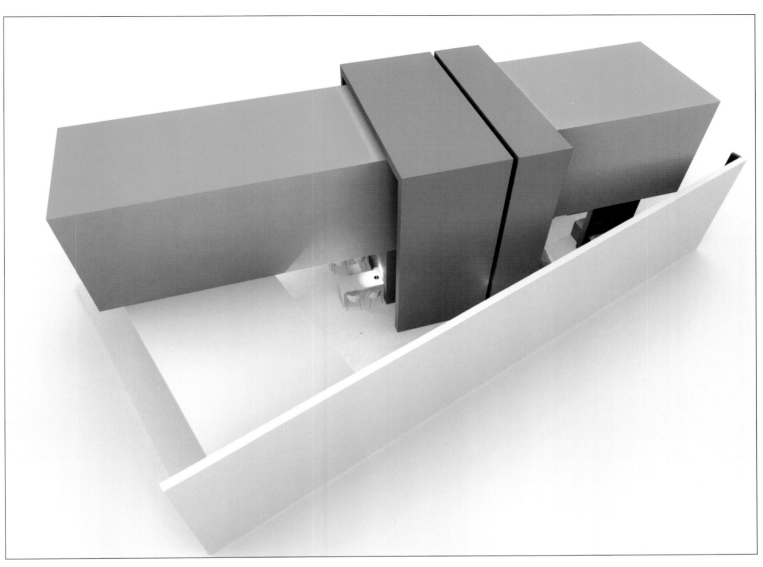

Mauk Design

Duncan Aviation

Located in Lincoln, Nebraska, Duncan Aviation is a company providing full maintenance service to the business jet industry. In the context of a trade show at which business jet manufacturers are showing off their latest multi-million dollar jets, getting noticed is a serious challenge.

Since Duncan Aviation and all their competitors utilize similar facilities and equipment, the designers decided to have the exhibit emphasize the importance of their highly skilled employees.

The display stand occupied a 40' x 50' island and was housed under a canopy consisting of 5" x 7" portraits of every one of Duncan's 2200 employees. These are the people who work over your aircraft. Each portrait was printed directly on sintra®, then slid over 1/4" stainless steel rods.

Their logo is instantly identifiable within the industry, so it was transformed into a glass and stainless steel sculpture in the center of the display booth. As you approach the center of the sculpture, all the parts come together to form the logo, just as all the parts come together to form the aircraft.

The illuminated outline of an aircraft traveled from one side of the overhead sky to the other.

The veneer desk illustrated Duncan's skill in aircraft interior cabinetry.

Ten airfoil shaped aluminum fin museum cases showed items from each of Duncan's ten divisions, (sales, parts, airframe, and engine maintenance).

At Duncan, exhibits are re-used over a long period. Each of the airfoil fins had already been used for 11 years in a previous Duncan display installation. A new coat of paint and new contents will prolong their use for another 5-10 years. The five illuminated logo signs were also recycled for use in the new exhibit.

The pattern on the wall behind the desk was taken from a map of the aircraft flight corridors over the US.

The back wall contained aircraft-shaped windows that showed the clouds passing by from a passenger's point of view, accomplished with 4 monitors, and a loop of stock video images.

CLIENT:
Duncan Aviation
LOCATION:
National Business Aircraft Association
Show, 11/2005, Orlando, USA
DESIGN:
Mauk Design
COST:
170,000 $
PHOTOGRAPHS:
Andy Caulfield

Quinze & Milan

Quinze & Milan, Extremis, Dark, Duvel Beer, Kvadrat Fabrics

Once again three friends join hands: Quinze & Milan, Extremis (outdoor furniture) and Dark (lighting). Two guests have joined them this time, Duvel beer and Kvadrat fabrics.

At the entrance of the famous Superstudios in Milan, a 7-meter high tent was erected, covering a surface area of 25 by 15 meters.

The theme was a base camp, a place for people to come back to. And that is what the public did. In 5 days, over 12.000 free beers were handed out, every night a party...

The pictures show the bar, viewed from the entrance, with a one-of-a-kind installation above. The polyhedral wire structure contrasts with the white walls and appears almost flat, like a drawing. Skilful spotlighting casts sharp shadows on the wall that mingle with the real shapes, creating an amazing play of light and shadow. The back wall is virtually transformed into a three-dimensional space. Likewise, the three dimensional objects become readable as drawings. Thus, the concept of design becomes an integral part of the display, and the spectator is made aware of the object's graphic quality within the space.

Strips of textile fabrics are festooned liberally over a long frame, inviting visual and tactile inspection and creating a barrier across the floor space that distributes the stand into differentiated areas. Each separate atmosphere is orchestrated for the optimal display of a particular set of items.

Over 2000 light bulbs were used in this installation, demonstrating a wide and versatile series of lighting options. The overall concept is by Arne Quinze. The installation was undertaken by Quinze & Milan contractors. As usual in Quinze and Milan's installations, the graphics were created by Glossy.

DESIGN:
Quinze & Milan
LOCATION:
International Furniture Fair, Milano, 2005, Italy
PHOTOGRAPHS:
Contributed by Quinze & Milan

EXTREMIS DARK · *Quinze & milan*

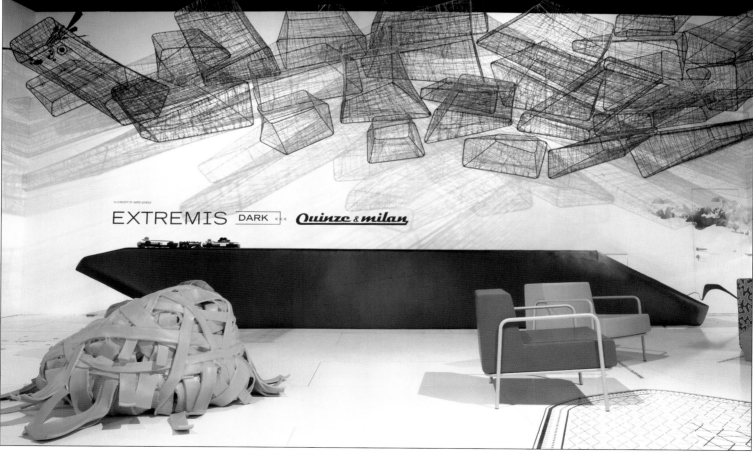

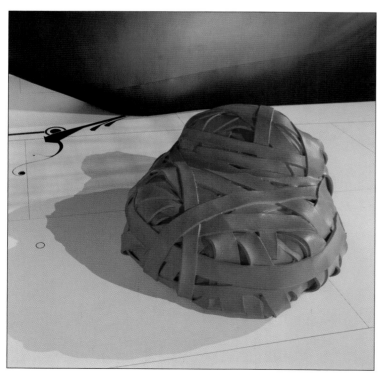

Zeeh Bahls & Partner Design

Rodenstock

Rodenstock is Germany's leading maker of spectacle frames and lenses. The strength of the brand lies in the successfully integrated summation of the components (dimensions) supplied to Rodenstock.

The "3rd. dimension" is the conceptual basis that determines the shape of the stand. Its architecture is intended to signify clearly that Rodenstock is the strong coordinating partner of a close professional network with their suppliers. Out of the 3 dimensions, 3 areas develop that present the visitors with three types of experience: " Active Partnership, Innovative Products and Individual Solutions "

The brief was to create three accessible spaces and clear, eloquent structures that would communicate the "Three Dimensions: Active, Innovative, and Individual ". A stage was required for presentations, in particular for the highlight theme "Sport". Moreover, the concept should illustrate the enterprise's international adaptability.

The initial concept from which this stands was developed was deceptively simple: out of 3 dimensions comes the Third Dimension

Three highly visible red cubes carry the three main statements of Rodenstock's presentation. These dynamic volumes visually transmit the three root concepts outward, enhancing a widespread perception of the brand's message, simultaneously defining three visitable spaces. Each "dimension" offers visual or spoken communications of that facet of the brand's products. The three spaces awaken the visitors' curiosity while creating a relaxed environment for communication to prosper, and ensure that people linger on the stand.

The suspended lightweight structure is completely clad in stretchable textile material that has been printed with very precisely interlocking designs, a technical challenge considering its geometrical complexity. Elastic textiles, PVC, glass, steel and metal sheeting in various forms and colors were used for this 499.5 sqm stand.

The first cube remains open in its full width, to serve as the main entrance that draws people into Rodenstock's 3 dimensional context.

Large format graphic walls follow the longitudinal axis of the central cube, in combination with the conversation desks. The exposed position of these desks is intentional, for clients to be welcomed and informed by the Rodenstock team as soon as they enter the stand.

Finally, an emotionally charged product display, attractive photographic installations, informative panels or even performances are used to present the novelties.

Rodenstock's presentation and display booth at theOPTI trade show, with its innovative products, concepts and services, was a trailblazing start for the following year. Besides the number of contracts signed during the trade show, invitations to subsequent trade shows and the aquisition of new clients gave a satisfactorybalance, rounded off in the immediate future, as new contacts made during the show were followed up.

Rodenstock's sales department recognized that they used the architectural statement of the stand as a working tool, to link the various levels of their work into a meaningful whole.

The stand-architecture created for OPTI 2006 was used for later shows in Milan and Dubai with minor adaptations. Its multiple

CLIENT:
Rodenstock GmbH
LOCATION:
OPTI 2006, Neue Messe München,
13- 15 January 2006
ARCHITECTURE:
Zeeh Bahls & Partner Design
CONSTRUCTION:
Zeeh Design Messebau GmbH
LIGHTING:
Luxoom
PHOTOGRAPHS:
Thomas Koller

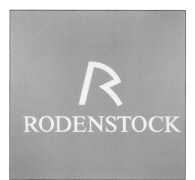

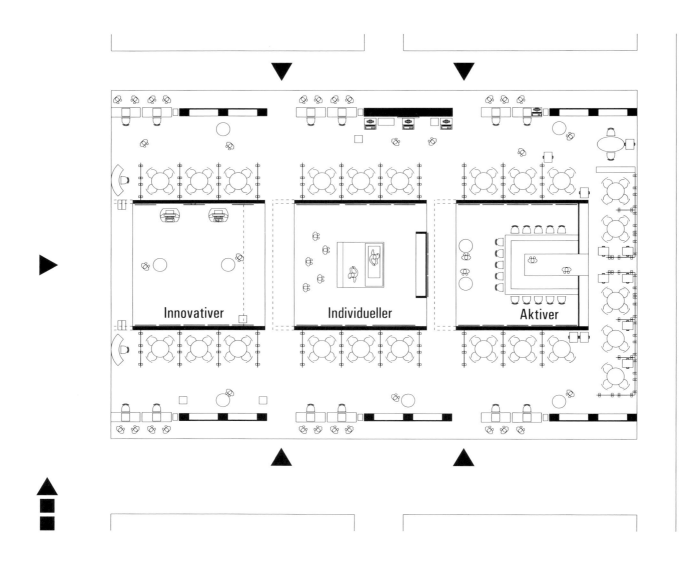

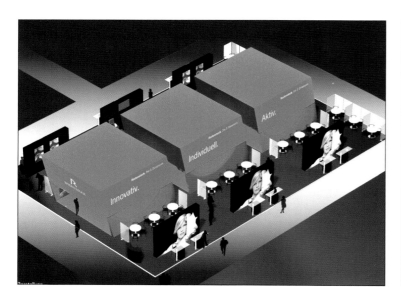

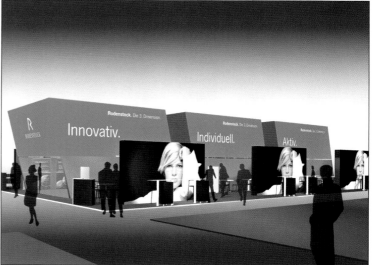

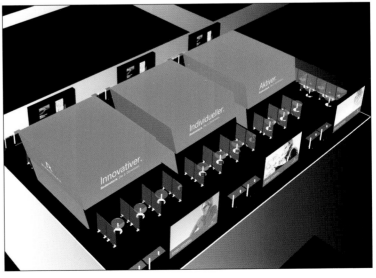

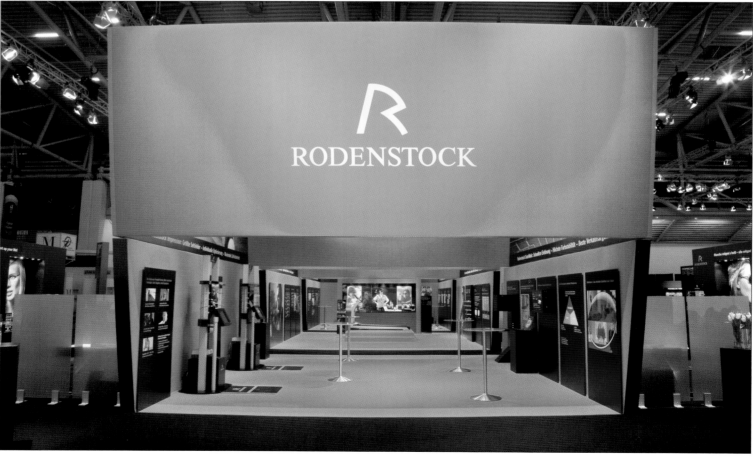

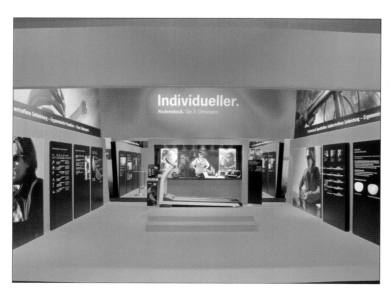

burdifilek

Teknion 2003

Toronto, October 2004 –. The change of seasons brought another interior design award for the team at burdifilek, this time for a dynamic exhibition design that infused a sense of fashion and excitement into an office environment. burdifilek was approached by the Teknion Corporation to create a sophisticated exhibition booth at the 2003 International Interior Design Exhibition in Toronto. The firm took a different type of approach to the client's booth concept and designed an unconventional corporate environment. The design incorporated a sense of high fashion into the typical 'office lifestyle' while highlighting the company's new European themed office line. The award was presented at the annual 'Best of Canada' ceremony at the Design Exchange on October 1, 2004

Using classic modernist forms with unexpected materials and finishes, a sense of drama permeates the design. High-gloss black lacquer combined with flesh-toned glass all play out under a lilac to skin-toned colour graded ceiling. Unexpected features include imported French black silk fringe and flesh toned wool carpet.

The booth structure was designed as a private showroom on the exhibit floor to promote the product line's flexibility within the office environment. The silk fringe insures the privacy of the space at the same time not impeding access to the showroom. The team designed modular components with intentional seams to disguise joints allowing for off site manufacturing and finishing, and on site installation. The ceiling system and lighting are a single free floating component independent of walls to minimize the installation period (trade show booths typically set up in 3 days). Lucite wall panels and fringe curtains also are detailed to fit in a slot system to allow for height adjustments.

Teknion's new furniture system debuts in black, white and lilac, unconventional and striking against a warm and expressive booth design. The overall concept represents Teknion's dedication to creativity and becomes a signature example of temporary architecture.

CLIENT:
Teknion
LOCATION:
IIDEX/NeoCon Canada 2003
ARCHITECTURE:
Burdifilek
PHOTOGRAPHS:
Contributed by Burdifilek

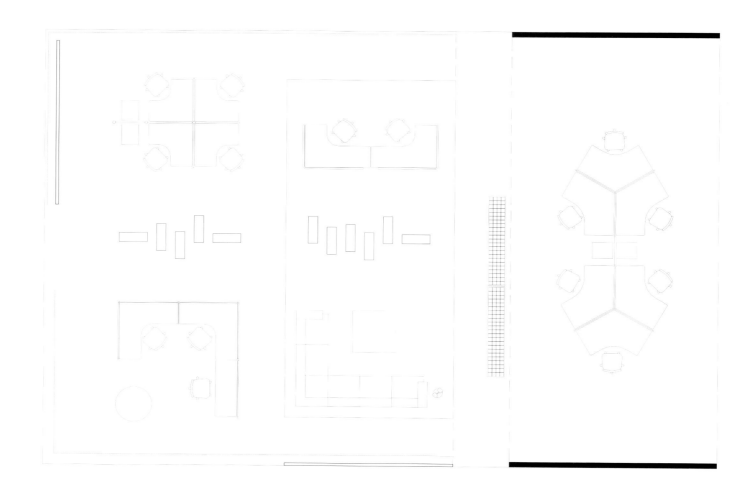

Christian Werner

Carpet Concept

Visitors to the Carpet Concept stand at Domotex were greeted by luminescent Barolo-red carpeting, fluttering above their heads, like flags. The contractworld section at Domotex offered a focused forum for information and presentations dedicated to project fit-outs. Moreover, it was here that Carpet Concept provided insights into their new ideas for contract carpeting.

Christian Werner fashioned the stand as an exclusively visual eye-catcher. Widths of woven carpeting from the LYN Collection traced wavelike movements on the walls and ceiling and constituted a moving (in every sense of the word) object of perusal. The LYN Collection by Peter Maly and Carsten Gollnik is made particularly alluring by tiny stainless steel fibers woven into the carpet pile, which casts a glimmering spell upon the bystanders. A succession of strict white rectangles defined the whole volume of the stand creating an austere grid. This framework was invaded by hovering and glimmering red waves, in a meaningful juxtaposition of functionality and sensuous play, the natural habitat of creativity. By linking this concept to the brand, the architect displayed the message that underlying this brand is the creative union of pleasure and function.

As the bewitched spectators peered into this ocean of carpets in motion, the stand's interior came into sight. Indeed, the space was invitingly open, facilitating many a profitable encounter during the show. Carpet concept wanted attention centered on Net, their latest woven product. With its innovative metallic visuals, the dynamic installation of the stand specifically underscored the more unusual characteristics of the line and, indirectly, the translucent spatial impact of new-age architecture. Its first appearance at Domotex fascinated prospective buyers, customers and the trade public alike.

LOCATION:
Domotex 2002
DESIGN:
Christian Werner Industrial Design,
Hollenstedt, Germany
PHOTOGRAPHS:
Soenne, Aachen; Office Christian
Werner, Hollenstedt

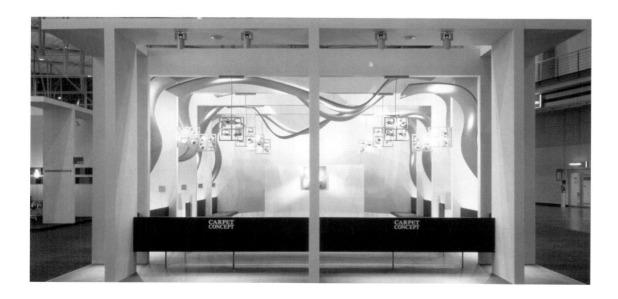

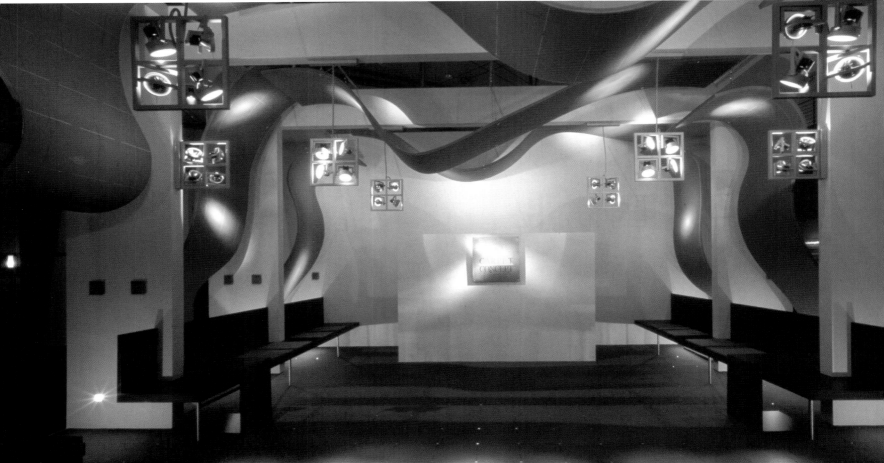

Michael Young

DuPont Corian®

Michael Young, a prominent name in British design created this unique stand for DuPont Corian®, the originator of solid surface in the 1960s. Corian® is strong, versatile and beautiful, it can be cut, carved, routed, inlaid and thermoformed into almost any shape. Easy to maintain and pleasing to the touch, its special bonding method results in apparently seamless surfaces. It comes in over 90 colors and textures and in certain shades and thicknesses it is translucent, making its applications limitless.

Michael Young had previously used Corian® for various projects, and is familiar with its possibilities, which he explored further within the theme of the stand, Light & Translucency.

Working with Katrin Petursdottir of M.Y. Studio in Iceland, Bill Holding of morph uk and Sheridan Fabrications, Michael Young has used CNC technology to carve graphic designs into a backlit wall panel of the material. Demonstrating its translucency, a glowing design magically lights up.

Katrin Petursdottir explains that her graphic work explores and expands the imaginary worlds she has cultivated since her childhood. With computer technology, the possibilities for expressing this world have become so detailed that its own kinetic momentum and its own life have developed. Applying this imaginary world to a solid material like Corian®, has given her the opportunity to explore depth and texturing, as opposed to printing.

Exploring the many possible options of modulating the translucency of Corian®, testing the materials response to different types of router bit at different depths, a multi-textured light patination has been created which shows great potential as a standardized form of wall-cladding.

The stand also displayed Michael Young's new seating designs: the "Holey Chair", made entirely of Corian®, exploits the strength and thermo-formability of this material to create gently curved seats, which are durable, non-porous and ideal for indoor or outdoor use.

CLIENT:
DuPont Corian®
LOCATION:
100%Design 2001, London, UK
DESIGN:
Michael Young
PHOTOGRAPHS:
Contributed by Michael Young Studio
ILLUSTRATOR:
Katrin Petursdottir

ozon - büro für ganzheitliche kommunikation

Bosch Siemens Hausgeräte

Bosch and Siemens are leaders in the field of small machines. Despite a widespread trend to steer clear of trade shows, BSH wanted to display its position in the market and use the show to make a mark on the 2005 scene. Each brand was to be spatially and visually sharply separated, yet a mutual unity (B/S/H) should occur, making their appearance as separate worlds, yet receiving a balanced amount of attention. Bosch is close to people, enhancing people's quality of life by means of technical competence. Bosch is a classic in the kitchen, hence the slogan "the technique of life", which a star-chef (Ralf Zacherl) will illustrate. Siemens is design and high-tech-lifestyle oriented, hence the slogan "the future is here to stay". Each brand would have about 150 sqm available for backstage meeting rooms, catering space and logistic areas. Each would present over 50 items. As all other spaces at the Frankfurt show were taken, BSH had to deal with a daylight-flooded, 32 m high atrium.

The challenge was to prevent the atrium's architecture and the changing natural light conditions from overpowering the communicative strategy. The architectural setting forced the two brands to be placed one after the other. Two large banners presented the two logos on either side of the access steps. This "portal" created a new space, framing the two brands. The different height available to each brand provided two distinctive contexts. The Siemens futuristic theme suggested the enclosure and artificial lighting of a "silvery spaceship"; Bosch was placed in a hovering "cathedral of enjoyment", bathed in natural light.

The Siemens mood is high tech and modern, Bosch is sensual and light. A chill-out lounge atmosphere predominates inside the space. Great oval windows line the walls, onto which landscape projections drift by, as if we were flying. The center has a Cosmic Cocktail Bar and presentation areas for the washing machines and vacuum cleaners. To illustrate the slogan "the future is here to stay", a sensor-steered cleaner-robot vacuums its way through a backlit landscape of vases, without knocking them over. Toasters and electric kettles hover as silhouettes in a mystical blue space. Under each item is a button that turns a white light-beam onto the product. After a couple of minutes the light turns automatically back to blue, giving all the products a futuristic touch.

The Bosch Cathedral hovers in the air, feather-light. In the center, the altar of pleasure is surrounded by 8 to 12 meter long translucent textile panels that reach to the sky, giving the installation an immaterial look. The textile panels and the spherical display modules only reveal their content when observed from the front, which opens a new perspective. The powerful direct sunlight is filtered and diffused on its way down, to enable the stand's lighting to be effective. Inside each display module, the products become unique, jewel-like objects, exclusive and quiet. Visitors embark on a voyage of discovery, which the textile panels guide. In the center, star-chef Ralf Zacherl cooks up secret delicacies while he fascinates the public with his cooking stories. Both stands are made of very light, low-cost structures and textile finishes, all of which are suspended from the hall's roof.

CLIENT:
Bosch Siemens Hausgeräte
LOCATION:
Ambiente 2005, Frankfurt, Germany
ARCHITECTURE:
ozon - büro für ganzheitliche kommunikation
PHOTOGRAPHS:
Contributed by ozon
www.ozon-team.de

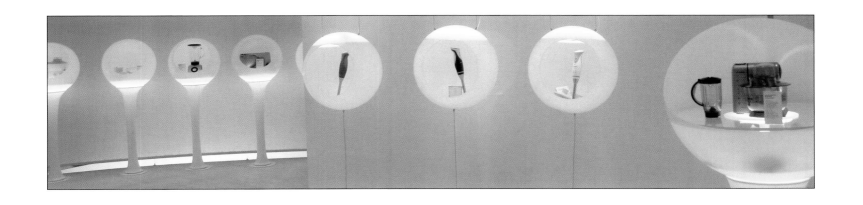

Schusterjungen und Hurenkinder GmbH

Adidas AG

For the Adidas stand at the OutDoor 2005 trade show in Friedrichshafen, the company's new presentation was developed on the basis of their slogan "LIFE IS OUTSIDE". Nevertheless, the slogan and even the company logo play a modest role in this display. Here, the work of bringing the visitors within range of the corporate message is left to the installation to resolve on its own. It is achieved by taking an unusual scene (a crowd of people all moving in the same direction) and raising it a conspicuous number of feet above the surroundings. Human curiosity is all that is needed to complete the strategy.

Nature can be represented by a surface of natural lawn; three strips of this material undulate through the air, dividing it into a space above and a space below, and making a subtle reference to the three strips of the Adidas logo. The space is then segmented further by introducing vertical dividers, towering walls reminiscent of a potentially oppressive urban skyline. These mark various boundaries between indoors and outdoors, distributing the space to suit various functions, looking, trying on, buying, but also sitting, talking, making business decisions. Thus, some areas have a ceiling above them, others do not, some are at a suitable height for people to feel comfortable standing inside, and others merely house the shelves or hangers with the company's products.

Walking, running or jumping along these linear grass hills, in correspondence to the three product lines of the Adidas outdoor range, a numerous congregation of mannequins, fully equipped by adidas for specific outdoor activities, advance dynamically towards the end of the stand occupied by the reception desk.

The floating grass paths raise the visual stage above the surrounding area, making the enigmatic scene visible from a distance. The logo's discreet presence makes it all the more certain that the visitor will come into range to discover what it all means. The installation portrays people as moved by an urge to leave the indoors. This urge is transmitted to the spectator through a simple process of identification. At that end of the stand, the reception desk and the adidas personnel are available to achieve a successful link up between the goal and the means. This is visualized through various video screens with emotional pictures of natural scenery, in which the brand's three stripes subtly appear.

CLIENT:
adidas AG
LOCATION:
OutDoor 2005, Friedrichshafen, Germany
ARCHITECTURE:
Schusterjungen und Hurenkinder GmbH
CONSTRUCTION:
Stagegroup GmbH
SURFACE:
2150 sqft (200 sqmt)
PHOTOGRAPHS:
Oliver Jung

LIFE IS OUTSIDE.

adidas

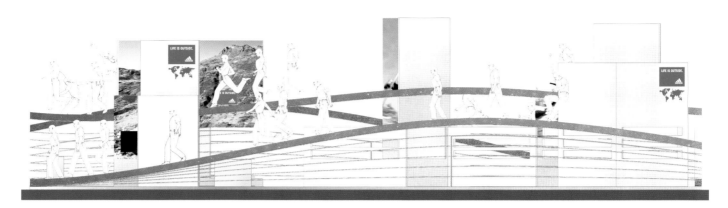

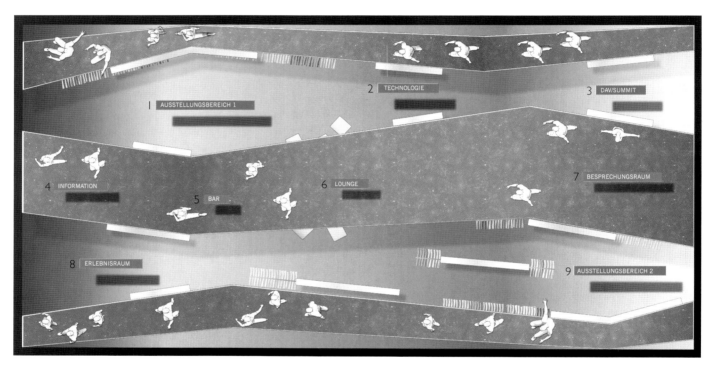

1. Exhibition area 1
2. Technology
3. Dav/Summit
4. Information
5. Bar
6. Lounge
7. Meeting room
8. Experience room
9. Exhibition area 2

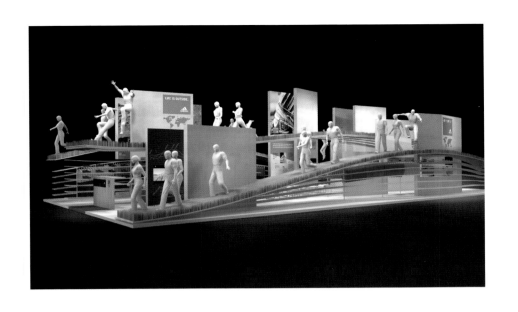

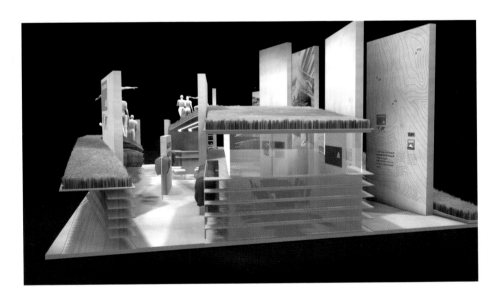

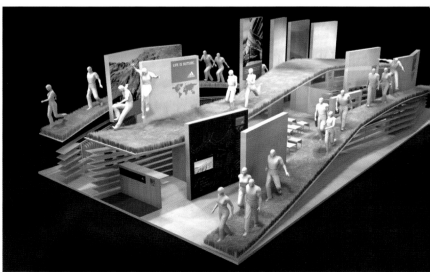

Ignasi Bonjoch

Biosca & Botey

The client wished to brand his identity as a significant lighting contractor at Construmat, Barcelona's main building trade show. The designer chose the idea of a black box pierced by a beam of light: no products, no lamps, no names, no makers. The idea at the back of this daring strategy was well expressed by the firm's manager: "At Biosca & Botey we sell ideas about light, we are consultants and designers. The products come as a result of this basic premise".

Ignasi Bonjoch, who had already designed the Biosca & Botey shops in various cities, proposed a 10m wide, 9m long and 3.5 m high box, painted in various shades of black anthracite, deep brown, intense black, matt black..., occupying the full 90 sqm of available floorspace. Two sides remained open; from the ceiling hung a circular luminaire, 6 m in diameter, with the company logo in black on white. Like a torch in the darkness, the logo projects an area of white light upon the black carpeted floor.

The great empty space is crossed by a 7m long counter, lacquered in red, to attend the visitors' requests, present projects and exchange ideas. Behind one of the side walls there is a small store room and a meeting room, simply separated from the outside by a red string curtain. A display niche was let into the full length of the other side of the stand, with images of the most significant projects realized by the firm.

The jury chose this project as the winner of the Ambit award to the best stand at Construmat 2005.

CLIENT:
Biosca & Botey
Proyectos de Iluminación
LOCATION:
Construmat 2005, Barcelona, Spain
ARCHITECTURE:
Ignasi Bonjoch
COLLABORATORS:
Guillem Hortoneda,
Marta Moliner (designers)
Anna Catasús (graphic design)
SURFACE:
970 sqft (90 sqmt)
COST:
28.000 €
PHOTOGRAPHS:
Eloi Bonjoch

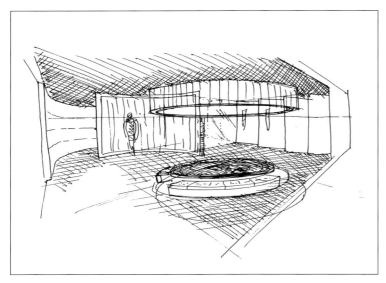

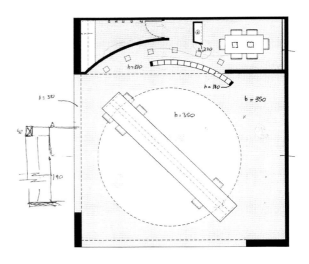

3deluxe

Mercedes-Benz (Future Mobility)

The pavilion designed by 3deluxe was first shown in Berlin, from where it traveled to the Mercedes Benz Center in Paris. The client wished the display to illustrate Mercedes-Benz' research into eco-friendly propulsion concepts.

The structure is cylindrical, a room within a room, a schematic three-dimensional rendering of environmentally neutral cycles. Thus, the visitors are drawn intuitively into the subject, as they move in circles suggestive of cyclically renewable energies.

The façade creates a futuristic impression, as rotating horizontal lines of light interact with darker areas, bringing the architecture to life, awakening curiosity, but unveiling only the title's three-dimensional lettering, integrated unobtrusively into the façade.

The façade's ribbed surface consists of rectangular champagne-colored anodized aluminum tubing. Attached to each of these sections are four cold cathode tubes lined up vertically, making a pattern of 336 individually controlled units. The narrow lights make the lines very delicate. The façade between them is lined with matt white Plexiglas paneling. Two wall elements, at different distances before the cylinder mark the entrances, through which a blue interior glow is glimpsed from the exterior.

Computer-animated video sequences are projected on 360° of the upper half of the inside wall, suggesting a flowing environment of color, enlivened with moving blue streaks and geometric moirés, a symbol of clean energy.

Questions such as "When will emission-free engines become reality?" or "Can I afford to run my car in the future?" float over the background, engaging people to seek for answers.

The central element is a floor-to-ceiling glass cylinder also used as a 360° screen. Here, the information projected over the background urges visitors to use the three interfaces, with which they can switch between the four main menus, "high-tech motors", "high-tech fuels", "hybrid engines" and "fuel-cell technology".

The touch-sensitive interfaces are mounted on a white leather bench that runs around three-quarters of the room. Three visitors can operate at any one time, while seven more can watch. The rest of the room between the two entrances is solely standing space. Detailed information is also accessible – the sub menu of each main menu contains three special interest films besides the main feature.

The interior atmosphere is defined by cool lighting and streamlined aesthetics, so materials with a warm look and touch were selected. Walls, floor and ceiling are covered in natural-colored woolen felt, with foam under the floor to soften it further. In contrast, white leather and brushed stainless steel introduce the vocabulary of automobile construction. The platforms for the vehicles and the information steles are coherently styled in coherence with the rest of the stand's characteristics.

CLIENT:
Mercedes-Benz
PROJECT:
Future Mobility –
Mobile Exhibition Pavilion for
Mercedes-Benz
LOCATION:
2005, Mercedes-Benz Center, Berlin
2006, Mercedes-Benz Center, Paris
ARCHITECTURE:
3deluxe
PHOTOGRAPHS:
Emanuel Raab

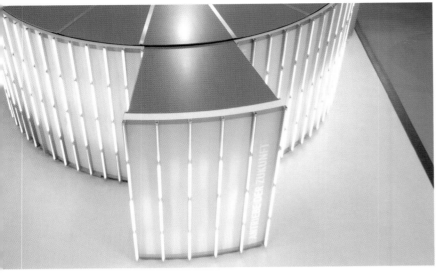

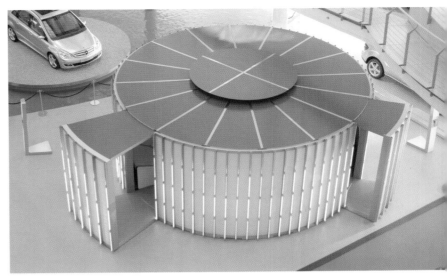

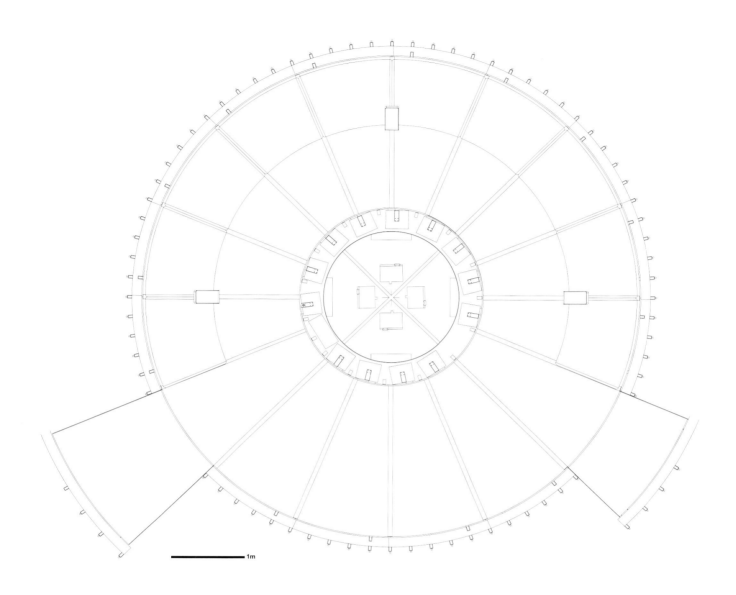

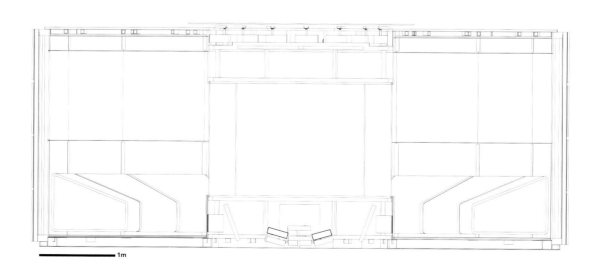

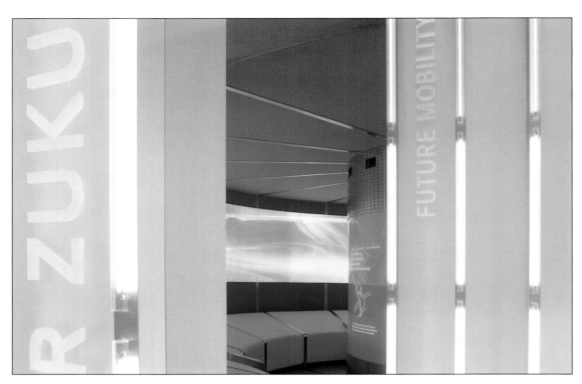

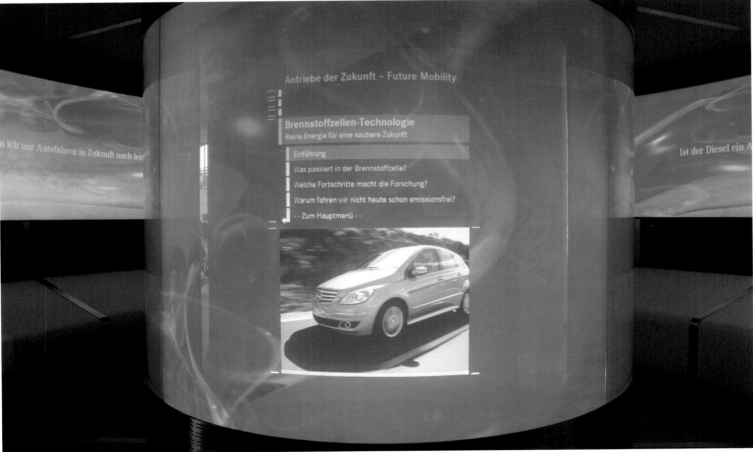

Zeeh Bahls & Partner Design

Siemens AG

At the Hanover Fair/Interkama+ 2006, the objective was to communicate that Siemens is the only partner who is at home with its products in all areas, from power distribution over the automation and field levels to MES/IT integration, can supply integrated, sector-specific automation and service solutions based on field-tested standard products and systems, and focuses on its customers and can show them new ways to increase the productivity of their companies. "Increase your productivity". The objective was to set in scene this core message. Three areas were created for the show: Products/Systems – The basis for all offers, Sector counter – Portrayal of sector competence using selected examples and Theme lounges – Entry via specific questions to cross-area topics.

Guided tours were intended to give visitors an overview of the place. The company's employees communicated to visitors the relationship between their tasks and the main idea of increasing productivity.

Some training courses were held during the show in cooperation with internal and external lecturers.

The idea was to develop a multi-level exhibition landscape similar to an arena which exuded both strength and clarity, producing a positive impact, and leaving a memorable experience. The products were presented at a focus point on the first floor. The conference lounges were located on the second floor, providing a suitable environment and infrastructure for talks. The third floor, which was made accessible by an escalator, served as entry point to a guided tour. A complete overview of the booth and the exhibited products was possible from this location. The front part of the booth was enclosed by a comprehensive, semi-transparent media façade intended to awaken the visitors' curiosity.

Due to the size of the booth and the limited amount of time to construct it, a two-storey prefabricated steel structure was designed and installed. The balustrades and ceilings were covered with a non-flammable fabric, and backlit.

To get approval for the first ever two-floor construction to be used at the Hanover Fair, a number of stringent conditions had to be fulfilled regarding escape routes and fire safety, particularly since the front portion of the booth was closed off by the media wall 90 meters long and 10 meters high. To reach the walkway on the third level, an escalator was installed in front as an added exit to the stairways.

The color choice was extremely important to the booth's effectiveness. The dominant color is petrol blue as used in the Siemens brand; the other tones were subordinated to it: achromatic anthracite, white, bright blue, green…

In the presentation show conceived by luxoom, an actor and an artist control the pre-recorded, 60 meter long, eight meter high LED/media wall, which is animated by graphic sequences that react to the movements of the actors and perform with them perfectly. Intense contrasting colors and large shapes illustrate the words of the moderator and emphasize them with movement, direction and speed.

On the second floor, the versa tubes (LEDs) on the product walls present an initial visual highlight for visitors looking out over the ground floor. On the back of the navigation walls, sector-related screens display a variety of media presentations. The harmonious lighting emphasizes the arena-like character of the stand. The business corner and the lounges are lit with particular care, by means of indirect lighting, and occasional spotlighting on visual points of attraction.

CLIENT:
Siemens AG / Automation & Drives
LOCATION:
Hannover Messe / Interkama+,
2006
ARCHITECTURE:
Zeeh Bahls & Partner Design
CONSTRUCTION:
Raumtechnik, Messebau & Event
Marketing GmbH
GRAPHIC DESIGN:
Publicis-Erlangen
LIGHTING CONCEPT AND
MEDIATECTURE:
Luxoom
PHOTOGRAPHS:
Körber Industriefoto GmbH

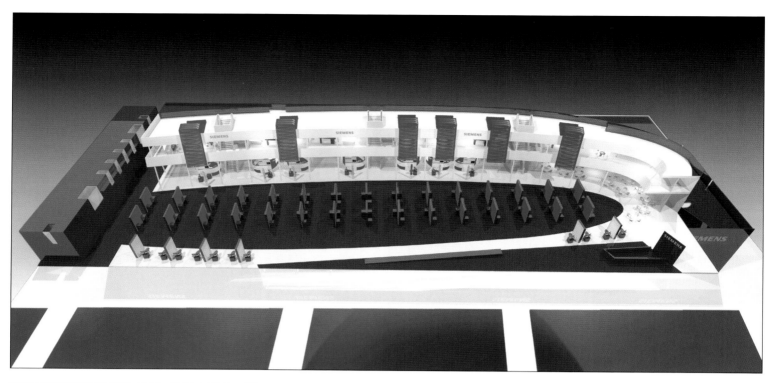

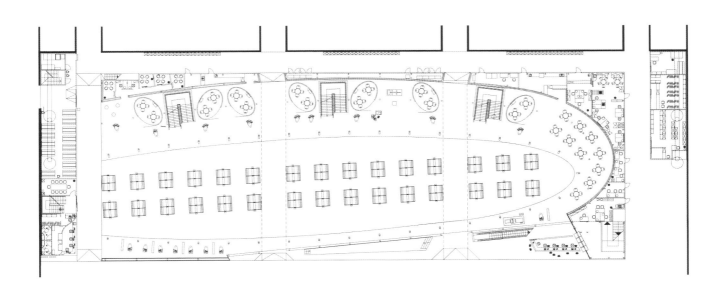

Kauffmann Theilig & Partner

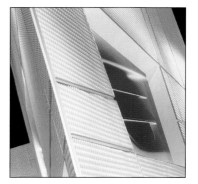

Mercedes-Benz

At the 2004 Paris Motor-Show Mercedes-Benz unveiled its four latest vehicles in a generous booth design that highlighted the new products.

The stand was located right in the north-west corner of Hall I. Stairs in front of the site restricted the view from the south. The visitors had to be clearly guided to the site. Ambition of the stand was a good distant effect as well as the definition of the stand as a „good site". That means the visual separation from the neighbourhood and at the same time an inviting openness. The main access emerged from the south-east corner following the main lines of sight and development of the stand.

19 vehicles were on display. Sub-spaces and different atmospheres had to be created with a clear communication strategy. Four impressive sharp-edged volumes, triangular in the floor-plan and spatially layered, simultaneously formed the space within the stand and contained in parts offices, storage-rooms and the restaurant. The surface of the volumes were wrapped in a skin of expanded metal in a silver tone. The volume's surface provided place for communication: there were showcases, projection screens and further vents integrated. Completed was the appearance of the stand by a structure of six horizontal lamellae (0,9m deep, 0,1m thick and 0,4m distance) at a height of 2,80m. They surrounded the entire stand and generated a partly transparent perimeter, which became more opaque as the visitor came closer. The lamellae were made of hard foam core with white veneer and were illuminated by integrated lighting on the upside. The lighting for the cars and the stand was integrated in the surface of the ceiling that was covered with an anthracite coloured drapery.

From the outside the elements created exiting views of depth. Inside the area of the stand is like an interior space that provides atmospherically a self-contained and remindable experience to the visitor. During the press conference one volume in the background served as the stage's backdrop. A stage, raised 0,3m above the visitors entry level permitted perfect visibility. After wards during the visitor-days all the 19 vehicles were in position.

The combination of materials and spatial elements presented a memorable atmospheric experience. That concept was very suitable to adopt it for other stands and to be enhanced for the changing conditions. So the lamella and the metallic volumes became the corporate appearance of Mercedes-Benz from 2004 to 2006 for many other stands.

CLIENT:
DaimlerChrysler AG, Stuttgart
LOCATION:
Hall I, Paris Expo, Porte de Versailles,
Mondial de l'Automobile Paris 2004
ARCHITECTURE:
Kauffmann Theilig & Partner
Freie Architekten BDA,
Ostfildern/Stuttgart
Project Manager: Martin Schroth
COMMUNICATION:
Atelier Markgraph,
Frankfurt am Main
STRUCTURAL ENGINEER:
form TL, Radolfzell
CLIMATIC CONCEPT:
Transsolar Enegietechnik GmbH,
Stuttgart
LIGHTING DESIGN:
Delux – Mediacampus, Basel
Schweiz
STAND CONSTRUCTION:
Ernst F. Ambrosius & Sohn,
Frankfurt am Main
PHOTOGRAPHS:
Andreas Keller, Altdorf

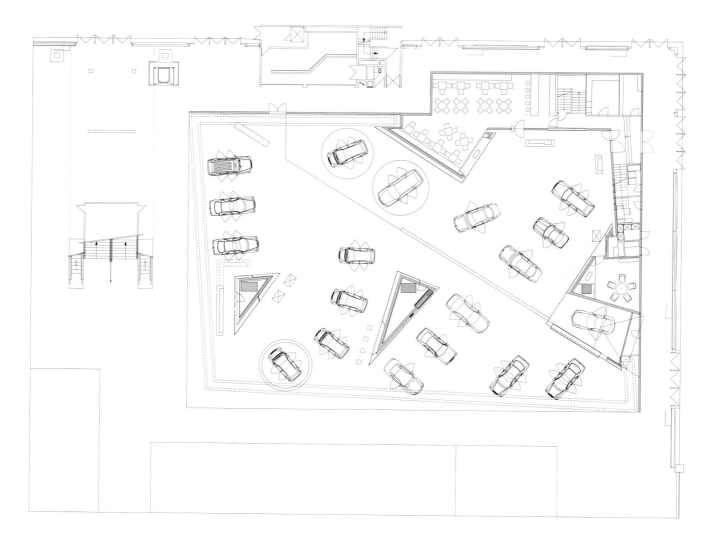

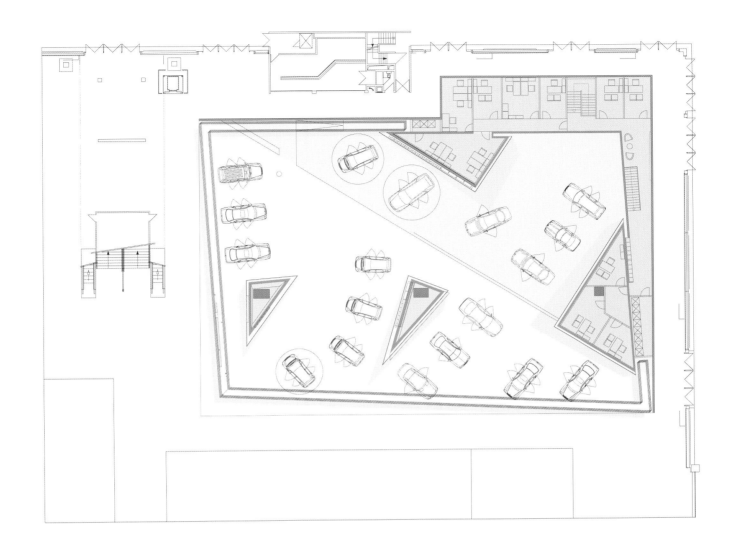

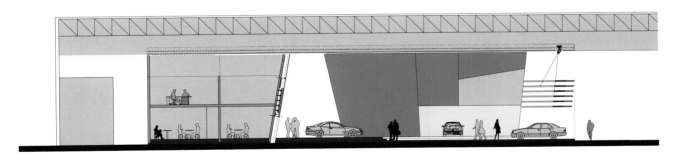

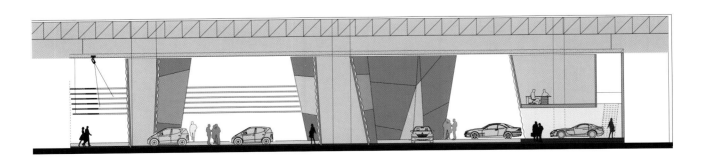

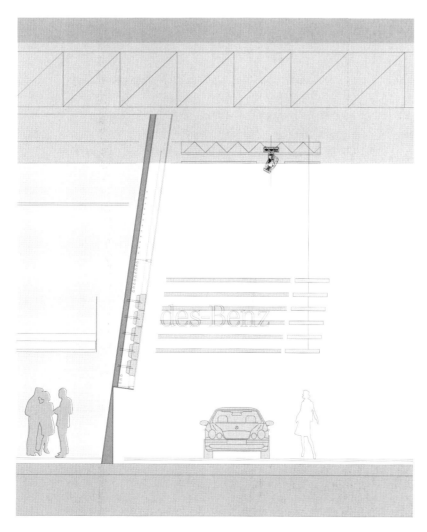

stengele + cie.

Heidelberger Druckmaschinen AG

At drupa 2004, Heidelberger Druckmaschinen AG presented itself as a global leader with a newly-defined strategic positioning. One of the most labor-intensive product shown in the world.

An appropriate infrastructure was needed for such a great project. The whole structure has been created with goals that were twofold: to send positive impulses to the printing and paper industry, and to effectively communicate, internally and externally, the company's strategic realignment as a partner to networked printers along the entire production chain of sheet fed offset printing. An appropriate infrastructure for such a great project.

To achieve these goals, architecture, graphics, media and realistic product presentations created a concentrated area for dialogue and a range of innovative solutions for print media on 7,800 sqmt of floor space. The clear allocation of space and functionality, supported by a graphics-based traffic system, gave the booth a lucid structure across two halls. The frequently-recurring red "clasp" provided a link element which symbolised both the integrative performance of Heidelberg as a one-stop solutions provider, and the company's partnership-based relationships with customers.

All construction elements (right down to the furniture) were variations on this theme, and derived their forms from it. Almost 2,500 spotlights, 350 computers and 18 kilometers of electrical cable, 300 m of compressed airlines for the exhibits, 120 speakers, 70 plasma screens and 30 cameras were part of the huge amount of elements needed for the installation and construction of this booth, basically built with wood, steel, attachments and paint.

Heidelberg has since applied the successful architecture and communication principles introduced at Drupa to its international trade shows, showrooms and facilities. This means the standards set by the Drupa presentation will continue giving shape to the image of the Heidelberg brand in years to come. One implementation was shown at print 05 in Chicago.

CLIENT:
Heidelberger Druckmaschinen AG
ARCHITECTURE:
stengele + cie.
COMMUNICATIONS:
Generators Communication GmbH
LOCATION:
Drupa 2004, Düsseldorf, Germany
PHOTOGRAPHS:
Contributed by Stengele + Cie.

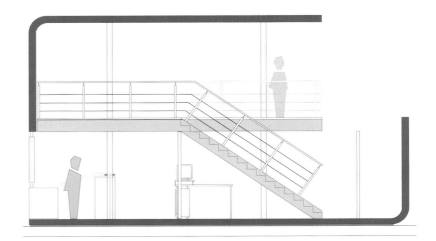

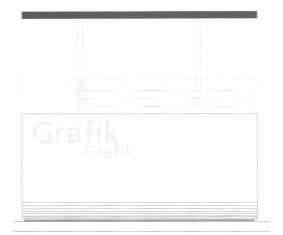

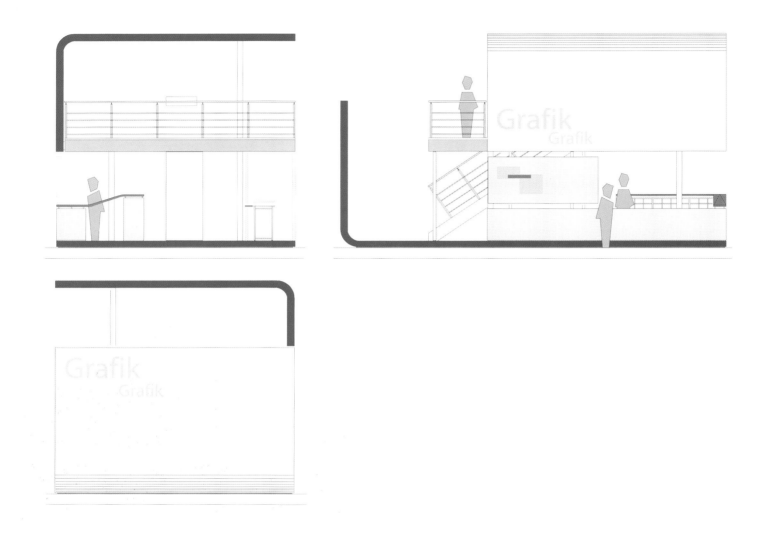

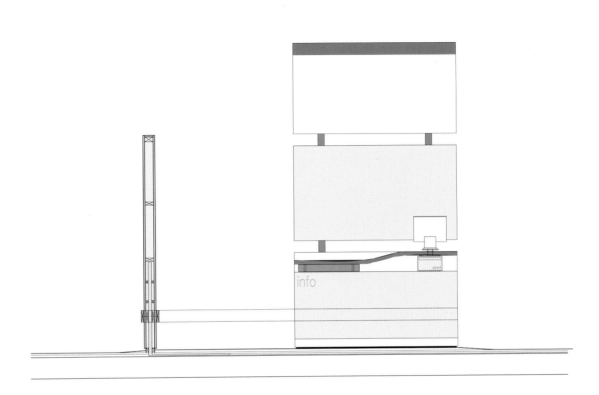

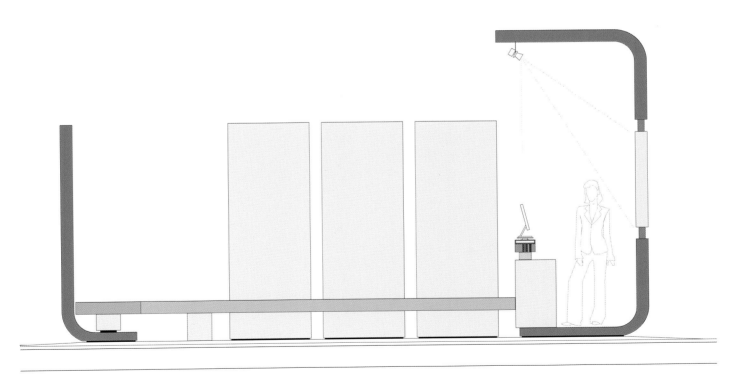

Coqi

L'Anverre is an art collective whose activities explore a wide variety of creative media, ranging from glass sculpture to photography, engraving, painting, and furniture design for the household or public space.

The design brief of the coqi project consists in the realization of a lightweight, humanly transportable, trade show display unit, capable of folding and dismounting into the minimum space, but providing a generous and inviting environment for commercial presentations. As an economically viable product, it aims at making participation in international exhibitions lighter and more flexible, opening these venues up to smaller enterprises, who can undertake the move like backpackers leaving for the mountains.

"Coqi" offers the possibility for a single person to set up the lightweight structure to cover 60 square meters of exhibition floor in as little as two hours.

A fundamental aspect of the whole concept required that the complete self-contained structure should not need additional fixing: a series of nine identical aluminum arches, each made out of three tubular elements, rotate around a central axis. This structure is then covered with a stretchable fireproof textile material. The complete set up operation can be carried out with no additional tools or particular building skills.

The cocoon-like shape of the structure is perfectly balanced, presenting a biomorphic appearance and creating a welcome relief from the generally overwhelming, square environments so characteristic of exhibition grounds and trade show architecture. The unit can be opened more or less to suit the needs of its user. Likewise, it can be drawn down to the ground, closing the unit completely when not in use.

CLIENT:
L'Anverre, Antwerp, Belgium
ARCHITECTURE:
Eer, Overijse, Belgium
Architects Geert Buelens & Veerle Vanderlinden
CONSTRUCTION:
Showtex, Antwerp, Belgium
FURNITURE:
De Noordboom, Ronse, Belgium
LIGHTING:
L'Anverre, Antwerp, Belgium
PHOTOGRAPHS:
Dario Tettamanzi

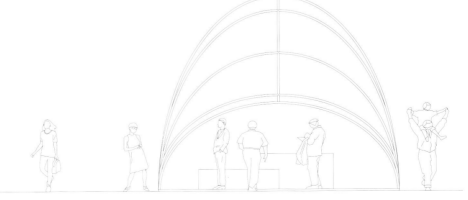

Grupo BH

Comex

The members of the architecture firm Grupo BH have authored a number of significant projects in America and Europe since 1999. With several trade show stands on their CV, their work has appeared in several books, specialized magazines, and in architecture-related exhibitions.

The exhibition stand that Comex commissioned for the Expo-CIHAC 2005 trade show in Mexico City, arises from the enterprise's need to communicate its know how in the field of finishes and coatings, in particular those of an innovative and specialized nature. Comex also offers educational courses at professional or DIY level to familiarize the public with the correct use of different coating applications and aesthetic choices.

The stand rests upon a pedestal that rises one step above the surrounding floor, defining the allotted floor space in the exhibition hall. The pedestal is finished with an impeccable coating of scratchproof, high-gloss white floor paint. This acts as the base for the seventeen curvilinear rings that form the outer shell of the constructed space.

The constructed space has a sculptural appearance, and consists of three interlocking volumes. Two of them, made up of three rings each, rest directly on the main floor at each end of the stand. The remaining rings are consecutively welded onto each other, generating a more elongated form that is supported upon the first two. Thus, a covered space is created on the ground level and a second space, for meetings, is contained on the level above. The floor between the two is supported by a barely perceptible steel structure. The interior surface of the walls exhibit seventy panels with different color finishes, with images of different uses and completed projects.

The continuity of the stand's formal characteristics and its neutral color create a balanced, low-key environment in which the multicolored products on display can cohabit to advantage with the architecture itself. The volume is a perceptible presence among the other stands and reads with sharp-edged clarity, but its rounded corners dispel a potentially aggressive look. The whole composition illustrates a harmonious fusion between the technologically advanced Comex coatings and a human dialog with the clients.

CLIENT:
Comex
LOCATION:
EXPO-CIHAC 2005 , México
ARCHITECTS:
Jorge Hernández de la Garza
Gerardo Broissin Covarrubias
COLLABORATOR:
Carlos Rubio Martinez
CONTRACTOR:
Grupo BH
PHOTOGRAPHS:
Paul Czitrom

111

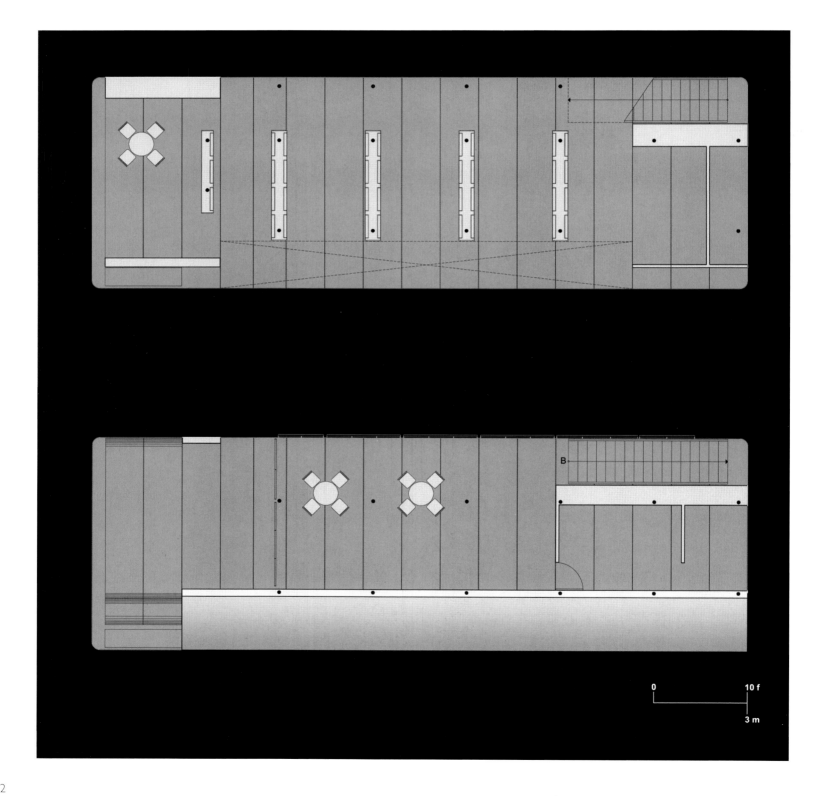

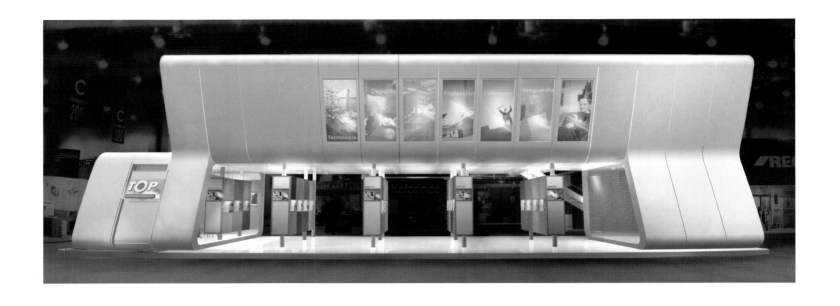

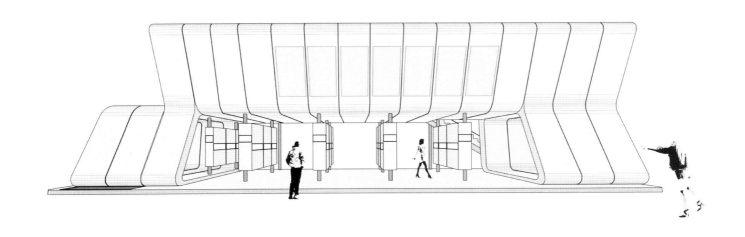

Gerry Judah

Ford Central

Ford commissioned a visitor exhibition to illustrate its contribution to personal and commercial transportation over 100 years and to showcase selected cars from its current range. Gerry Judah won the work against several top exhibition contractors including Britain's largest and best-known company in this field.

The confines of a 40m x 25m floor space made it difficult and costly to show a selection of the company's cars from the past 100 years, an inadequate and selective picture of Ford's heritage. Judah decided that a much more comprehensive story could be told with the use of scale model cars, backed up by audio-visual displays and a selection of "state-of-the-art" full-size passenger and competition cars.

After calculating that about 200 models on individual plinths and some 6 real cars would allow all-round viewing by a large number of visitors at any one time, Judah's curator started to track down models from Ford's 100 years, from early Model Ts and As up to the current range. Models of commercial, utility, and military vehicles were included, sourced from Britain, America, Europe, and the rest of the world. Ford's legendary competition history was also represented, from a rare model of Henry Ford's first race car up to diecast models of the latest race and rally machinery.

Three sizes of pointed ovoid section plinths were designed, each in a range of three heights. Models were individually wired to black bases and secured to the plinths, then covered with clear Perspex covers marked with the model year and name.

The plinths were finished in silver/grey and equally spaced throughout the exhibition area, which was dressed and carpeted in Ford's corporate blue. A matrix of pin-spots was installed overhead, one light immediately over each plinth, to create an intimate, involving atmosphere. The full-sized cars were spaced randomly among the models.

A backdrop around three sides of the exhibition was divided into ten sections, one for each decade. Each section featured text and graphics relating to Ford products, achievements, and activities in that decade.

Film footage from Ford's archives was edited together with footage of significant events of the 20th century to provide some 12 minutes of film. A specially commissioned soundtrack was added, and the film shown simultaneously on ten flat panel TV monitors, each centrally positioned in one of the 10 decade sections.

The exhibition was visited by a high proportion of the 158,000 attendees at the Goodwood Festival of Speed, and acclaimed as "best exhibition at the Festival" by event organizer the Earl of March.

CLIENT:
Ford
LOCATION:
Goodwood Festival of Speed, 2003
DESIGN:
Gerry Judah
PHOTOGRAPHS:
Contributed by Gerry Judah

Kauffmann Theilig & Partner

Mercedes-Benz

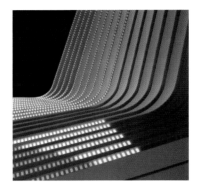

The swinging lamellae figure became a memorable symbol, a powerful image for the stand of Mercedes-Benz within the framework of the IAA 2003. Many sub-spaces emerge behind the unifying figure: The brand and their different product series.

A exhibition circuit guided the visitor through the stand top down. This circuit is marked by different spatial atmospheres that affected the dramaturgy of the stand: First there was the overview of the model range, then the theme-rooms came up behind the curtain of lamellae and in the end there was the highlight of the show – the new SLR – in the centre of the hall. From the entry of the hall the visitor is lifted by an escalator at the beginning of the main show to the height of 16,4m. From there a spiral pathway leads three full circles counter clockwise back to the starting point. A series of sub-spaces are excit-ingly developed along the way, in an ordered sequence that at no point seems forced.

The figure and the facade had been designed that the visitor alternately perceived details and the whole stand at the same time. The visitor starts on level 3 with an overview of the model range of Mercedes-Benz with occasional open views towards the highlight on the ground-level. On level 2 and 1 there are the theme-rooms: behind the lamellae the half closed facade concentrated the attention to the theme-world and at the same time the visitor didn't lose it's bearings while he had still a view of what is to come. Focused views are a preparation for the show's climax. Arrived on level 0 there's the presentation of the show's highlight: the visitor is totally surrounded by the lamellae-structure that seems nearly closed because of the inclined perspective on the structure.

Communication and light were supporting the effect of the spatial parts and the dramaturgy. The lamellae-facade is shaped like floating curves and on the front side of the lamellae there is a LED-surface installed that could be used as one big display. Communicational intentions were interfered through this surface and at the same time the facade began to breath and the space was dramaturgically rhythmized. The facade is open or closed according to the point of view – the views are orchestrated by the chosen gap between the lamellae. Each lamellae is 70 cm deep and is conical shaped: 2,5 cm thick on the inside and 10 cm thick on the outside. So the view was opened to the outside and the centre of the hall. In some parts the lamellae, upholstered in leather, became a balustrade window sill that invited the visitor to linger.

The endeavour to solve constructional and technical inventions are masked for the bene-fit of a integrated effect and a memorable design. The stand was awarded with international prizes.

CLIENT:
DaimlerChrysler AG, Stuttgart
LOCATION:
International Motor Show 2003
(IAA) Festival Hall, Messe Frankfurt
am Main, Germany
ARCHITECTURE:
Kauffmann Theilig & Partner
Freie Architekten BDA,
Ostfildern/Stuttgart
Project Manager: Udo Jaschke
COMMUNICATION:
Atelier Markgraph,
Frankfurt am Main
GRAPHIC DESIGN:
Design Hoch Drei, Stuttgart
LIGHTING DESIGN:
TLD Planungsgruppe GmbH,
Wendlingen
STRUCTURAL ENGINEER:
Pfefferkorn Ingenieure, Stuttgart
CLIMATIC CONCEPT:
Transsolar Enegietechnik GmbH,
Stuttgart
STAND CONSTRUCTION:
Ernst F. Ambrosius & Sohn, Frankfurt
am Main
PHOTOGRAPHS:
Andreas Keller, Altdorf

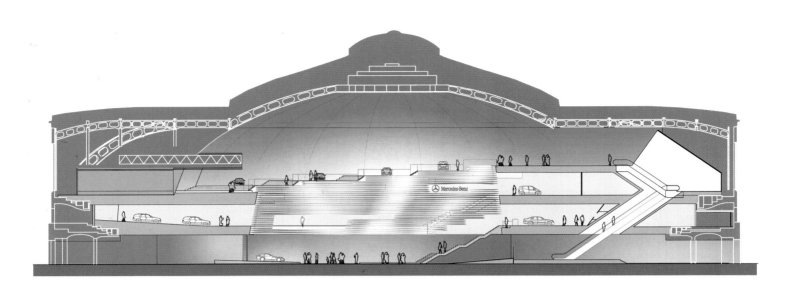

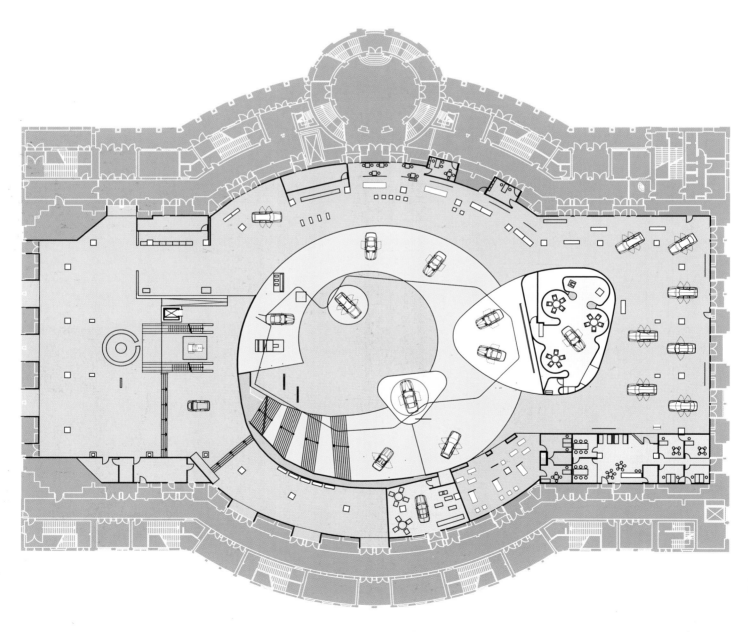

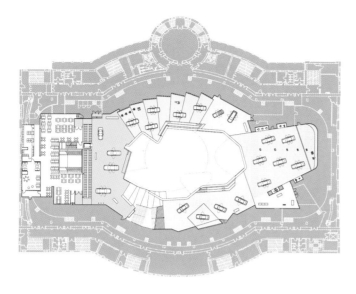

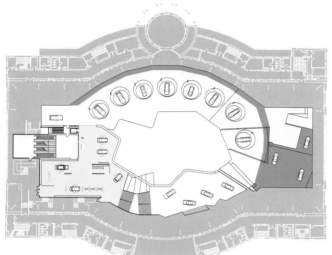

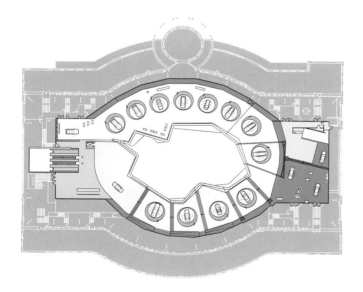

i29 office for spatial design

Vuurwerk

This fair stand was made for a young internet service company. A profile of this company was made by i29 to use this as a starting point for the concept. Vuurwerk was an internet service company that was rapidly grown from a small business into a large concern. Referring to the garage they started working, our keywords where under construction, hackers, rough. 'Vuurwerk' stands for fireworks, this fair stand had to crack!

By visualizing the word 'internet' into a tangible design, i29 made a large object with tentacles sticking out, like a living organism. As a machine, producing the product of internet on the spot. This lead to one big red object, integrating computers, meeting room and a bar, is placed on a high-gloss HPL floor. Around this internet machine, a landscape of white cubical shaped objects of different sizes can be used to sit on or stand along. Twice a year this stand is being used in the biggest ICT fair of the Netherlands.

The fair stand is divided into different zones and every zone has its own function; hanging around the bar, sitting or standing at your computer desk, or having a conference at the meeting booth. The structure of the design is open and easy to enter. The stand had to show off in its surrounding and competitors; big, powerful and shameless. The high gloss white floor bound the domain of 'Vuurwerk'. A surreal landscape of white cubical objects has the size and function of a seating, table or storage space. The world of 'Vuurwerk'.

This project was nominated for the Rotterdam design prize. An exhibition at the Boymans van Beuningen in Rotterdam, the Netherlands was held.

CLIENT:
Internet Provider Vuurwerk
LOCATION:
Boymans Van Beuningen, Rotterdam, The Netherlands, 2004
PROJECT TEAM:
Jaspar Jansen, Jeroen Dellensen
SIZE:
± 100 sqm
PHOTOGRAPHS:
Contributed by i29

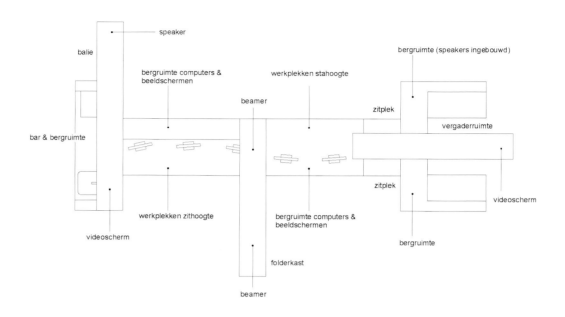

speaker

balie

bergruimte (speakers ingebouwd)

bergruimte computers & beeldschermen

werkplekken stahoogte

beamer

zitplek

vergaderruimte

bar & bergruimte

videoscherm

werkplekken zithoogte

bergruimte computers & beeldschermen

zitplek

videoscherm

folderkast

bergruimte

beamer

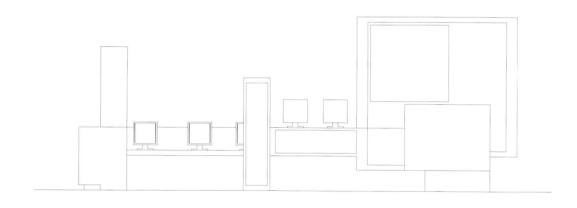

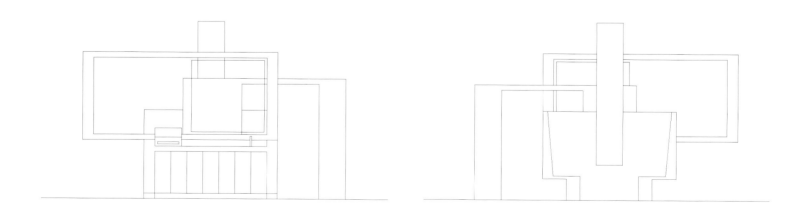

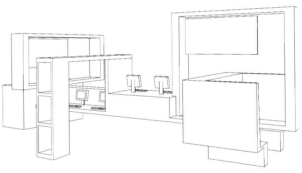

Limit architects

Umdasch Shopfitting Group

We all live in a consumer world; a world of extremes. The Umdasch Shopfitting Group used this global idea of our contemporary world of consumption to represent their project in the Euroshop trade fair 2005. The main concept was to communicate a concrete message to consumers about how shopping trends define demand, about global consumption of products all over the world. The polarization between luxury and discount is leading to an ever-increasing gap between opposite trends in shopping behavior, one focused on quality and individuality, another targeting the broad area of mass consumption. Thus, according to the philosophy of the Umdasch shopfitting group, for a world player today it is no longer the competition between products that is decisive, but the competition for visibility. This visibility awareness generally takes place at the sales venue itself. It is very significant for the consumer to be attracted by the product: only positive concepts with a clear and easily distinguishable profile can survive today in the excessively stimulus-satisfaction-oriented competition.

The Umdasch shopfitting group delivered a convincing argument for this philosophy with their trade fair stand at Euroshop 2005 in Düsseldorf. On a floor area of 918 sqm, six selected examples from their range were used to offer potential customers a demonstration of how sales areas can be made more productive and lucrative by uncompromising store branding, razor-sharp positioning and credible visualization of all facets of the strategy and concept. Different areas were designed for the products to be shown: as the client entered the stand, there was a group of six innovative tables; another small space contained four cross-like tables; a large cocktail bar was located at the end of the huge space, plus two more bar-restaurant areas on either side of the bar. Big graphics at the entrance of the stand achieved the targeted visibility. For the first time ever, the Umdasch Group presented the complete range of services offered by the different brands of the group (Umdasch shop-concept, shop-consult by Umdasch, assmann shop design). With this architectural statement, the European market leader in shopfitting underlines its aim to be a central player with lofty design aspirations and a portfolio of services and companies tailored to meet the growing demand.

CLIENT:
Umdasch Shopfitting Group
LOCATION:
EuroShop, 2005, Düsseldorf
ARCHITECT:
Limit architects, Vienna
GRAPHICS/COMMUNICATION:
section.d, Vienna
REALISATION:
Umdasch Shop Concept / Assman
LIGHTING:
Imagic Productions, München
SIZE:
920 sqmt
PHOTOGRAPHS:
Limit architects/section.d

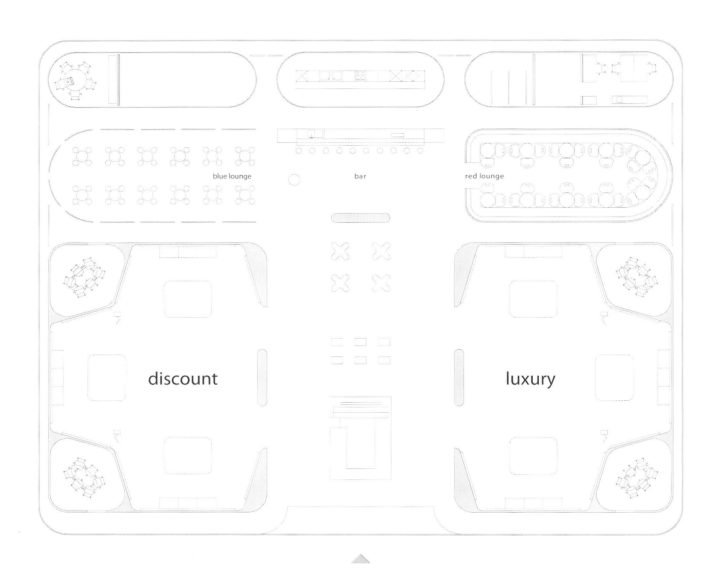

blue lounge　　　　　　　bar　　　　　　　red lounge

discount

luxury

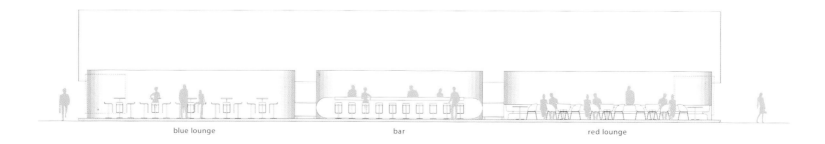

blue lounge　　　　　　　　　　bar　　　　　　　　　　red lounge

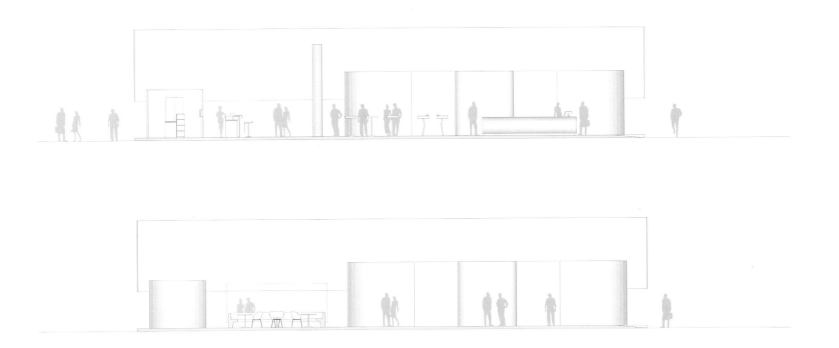

Maurice Mentjens Design

Count-it

The innovative design for this fair stand was created for Inbase's Count It cash desk systems during 2002.

All the dimensions of the booth and its set up were organized to be completely variable, as if one was in a moody changeable space. The I-Mac 'Count It' cash desk system was especially developed by Apple computers. All the cash desks are I-Mac computers.

One single material was used throughout the construction of this stand, matt Plexiglas: the material with which the I-Mac computers are made; white plastic, changes considerably under the influence of colored lighting, the material seems to have a chameleon-like capacity to alter its pigmentation. As a result, these changes altered the apparent nature of the whole place.

To enter the booth, which looked like an animal cage, one had to walk through a curtain of stainless steel tubes, suspended from the ceiling and hanging all the way to the floor. Each tube contained a strong magnet, fixed at the bottom end, so whenever a visitor drew the curtain to enter the stand, the tubes quickly swung back to their original position. All the materials used for the construction of this cage were white: the I-Mac computers, the desks and the sofa with polyurethane coating. Besides the large mirror wall located at the front of the cage near the entrance, only the floor preserved its natural steel color. The mirror enlarged the cage-like effect the visitors leaned through it to see the show. On the left hand side of the reception area there was a separate room for storage. Enclosed within another wall of steel tubes, another computer was placed upon a truncated pillar. This time the tubes were closer to each other. Above this curtain, there was a big screen on which graphic communications appeared. The command 'Count It' was reflected on the wall at the side. Next to A small kitchen unit ws provided in a space next to the storeroom.

A good sense of color and a rigorously homogenized choice of materials were implemented to achieve the communicative effect of this magnificent stand.

CLIENT:
Count-it
DESIGN:
Maurice Mentjens Design
PHOTOGRAPHS:
Bert Janssen

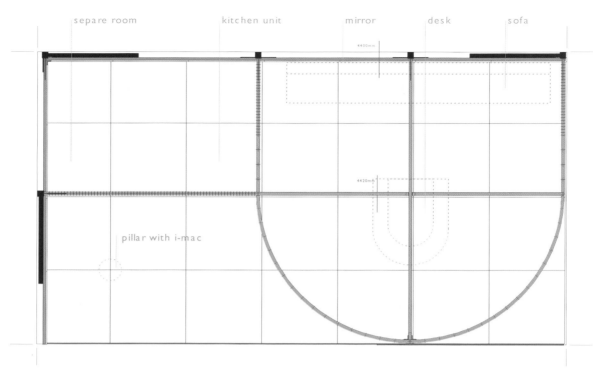

separe room   kitchen unit   mirror   desk   sofa

4400mm

4420mm

pillar with i-mac

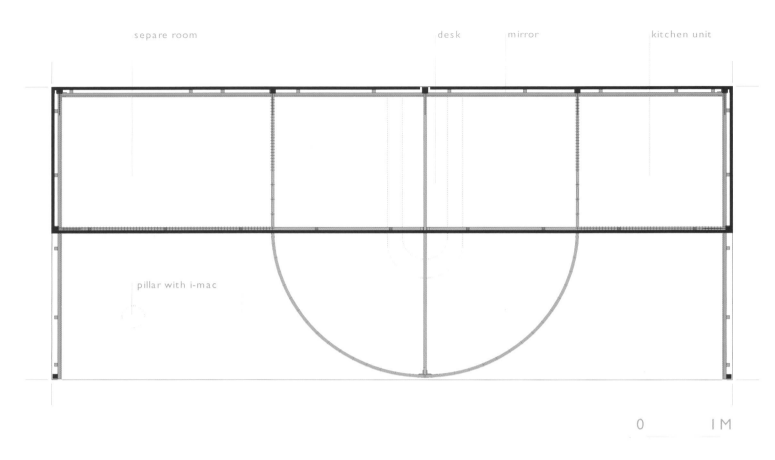

separe room   desk   mirror   kitchen unit

pillar with i-mac

0   1M

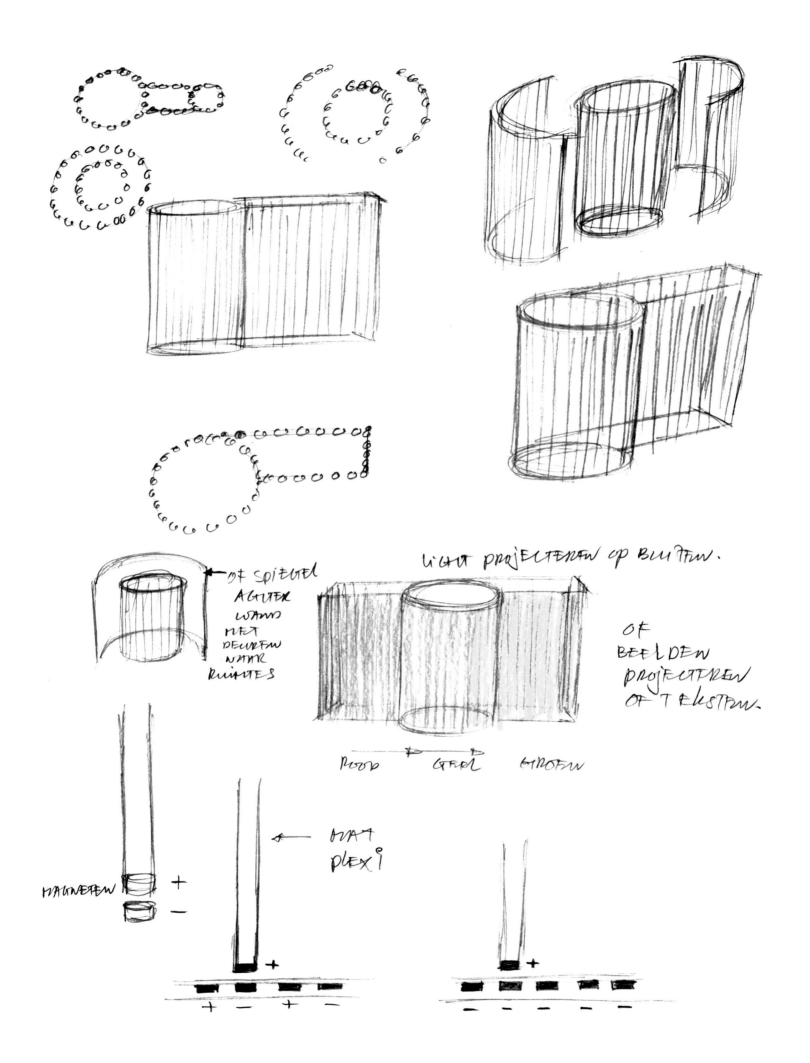

OF SPIEGEL
AGHTER
WAND
MET
DEUREN
NAAR
RUIMTES

LIGHT PROJECTEREN OP BUITEN.

OF
BEELDEN
PROJECTEREN
OF TEKSTEN.

ROOD   GROL   GROEN

MAT
PLEX?

MAGNETEN   +
              –

              +

+   –   +   –

              +

Schmidhuber + Partner

KPMG

"Numbers are alive," stated a member of the KPMG board. "Numbers tell us about the health of an enterprise we are analyzing, its background, and its future possibility to improve. It is very thrilling and requires a detective's instinct for clues. It is a passion shared by few, similar to a designer's love of proportions".

This suggested the concept of ordering binary numerical series on different surfaces and objects, so that words and statements could be interpreted. "The urge to penetrate the mystery entertains the spectator, awakening the desire to understand.

The installation created for the well-known business research and consultancy firm KPMG became one of the icons of the CeBIT 2000 Trade Show, and received the FAMAB Adam Award to stands under 150 sq.m. (1610 sq.ft), as well as the iF Design Award in silver. The stand occupied 75 sq.m. at floor level, plus 28 sq.m. on the floor above. All the press, from the Financial Times to TAZ, dedicated enthusiastic headlines to the design, the result of a highly successful cooperation between the KMS-team and the architects Schmidhuber & Partner.

A meaningful and visually exciting image of modulated transparency, the matt glass outer skin transmits a lively and many-layered visual message, in which the binary numbers 0 and 1 are the exclusive factual items of the display, while orchestrated light effects modulate the transparency. Mixing various layers of information generates moiré effects that vary with the spectator's point of view.

The visitors are the actors, in this choreographic interaction of people and digital codes. As spectators walk along the corridor, their vague silhouettes are projected into the flowing binary stream, creating a meaningful image of interaction between digital processes and living human beings. The clarity and intensity of the symbols plant KPMG's slogan "It´s time for clarity" securely in the visitor's memory.

Visibility equals value: the slogan and the design represented the firm not only at the CeBit show but afterwards, in a variety of places and contexts. The modular system makes it a flexible solution for surface areas between 12 and 100 sq.m. Embodying a meaningful expression of KPMG's identity and strategy, the representational elements are active. When expression and reality are brought together as here, the noticeable effect is easily assessed by the level of attention of clients, spectators and media.

CLIENT:
KPMG
LOCATION:
CeBit 2000, Hannover, Germany
ARCHITECTURE:
Schmidhuber + Partner, Doris Eizenhammer, Thomas Hanzalik
CONCEPT AND COMMUNICATION:
KMS, München: Michael Keller, Dr. Peter Gunzenhauser, Xuyen Dam, Michael Schuster, Eva Rohrer
REALISATION:
Ambrosius, Frankfurt a. Main
SIZE:
75 sqmt ground floor,
28 sqmt first floor
PHOTOGRAPHS:
Contributed by Schmidhuber + Partner,

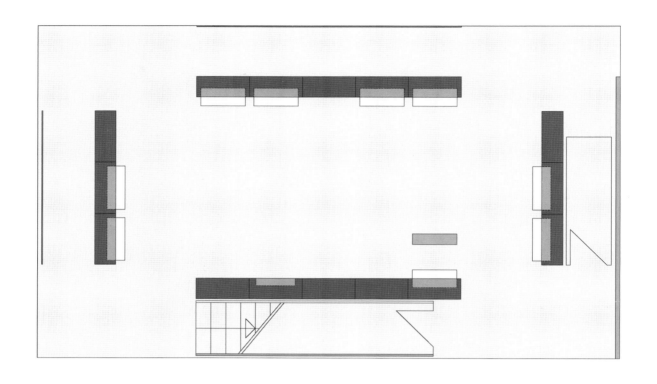

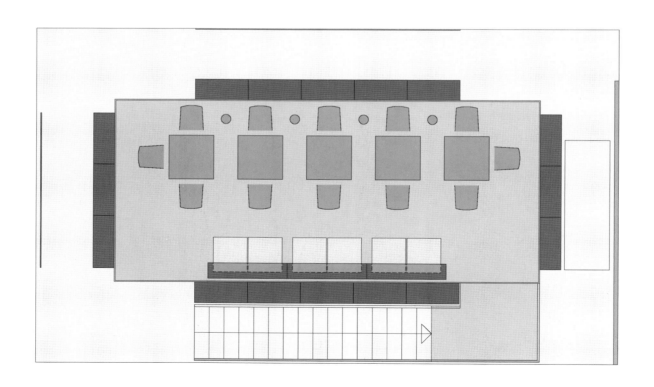

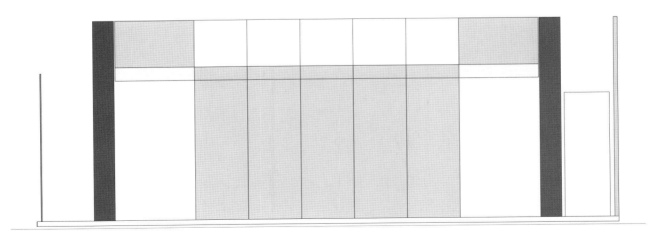

Walbert-Schmitz

LK Aktiengesellschaft

The Walbert-Schmitz design team followed the client's briefing and the stand was inviting. The 1614 sq. ft. space was distributed in three areas-, EXHIBITION, EVENTS and POS/ARCHITECTURE — each with its own designated colors of blue, orange, and green. These foundational business pillars were symbolized by three oversized tubes which had a significant influence on the stand architecture, where emotionally appealing film sequences were displayed in area-specific colors utilizing a catalyst-controlled rear projection screen.

Across from the tubes, specially conceived "View Panels" were positioned, upholstered in the colors consistent with the overall design of the stand. Visitors were invited to lean against them, to watch the films from a reclined position. A soundscape of chirping birds, wind, rain and ambient noises accompanied the presentation and augmented a relaxed atmosphere. This relaxing forum provided an excellent backdrop for the initiation of conversation with visitors.

The stand area was predominantly white, as a canvas for the brands identifying colors blue, orange, and green. Sufficient space was left over for furnishing elements in comprehensive CD/CI red, including the LK Branding, seating elements and table decorations. A coherent color-range was integrated into every detail, such as invitations, fruit drops, and sugar for coffee give-away souvenirs — the marketing and furnishing concepts were thought out as a unit.

A long white back-lit bar counter defined one side of the stand and invited visitors to conversation. On the other side, a waist height, organically formed discussion table was positioned. Visitors were tempted to relax, sit and chat. Two meeting rooms were available in the stand areas enclosed at the backs, for deeper business discussions. The upper area was bounded by a fabric sheet ceiling, which reflected brilliant white light. A six meter high back wall with its brilliant white finish displayed the LK company logo, visible even from a distance.

On the outside surface of the previously mentioned "View Panels", a product innovation from VERSA TILE acted as an eye-catcher for people and visitors passing by. Its 1 billion displayable colors continuously attracted interested visitors to the stand.

CLIENT:
LK Aktiengesellschaft,
Lichtdesign & Klangkonzept ,
Multimedia Praesentations Systeme,
Essen Germany
LOCATION:
Euroshop 2005, Duesseldorf,
Germany
REALISATION:
Werbe- und Messebau Walbert-
Schmitz GmbH & Co. KG
PHOTOGRAPHS:
Axel Stoffers, Essen

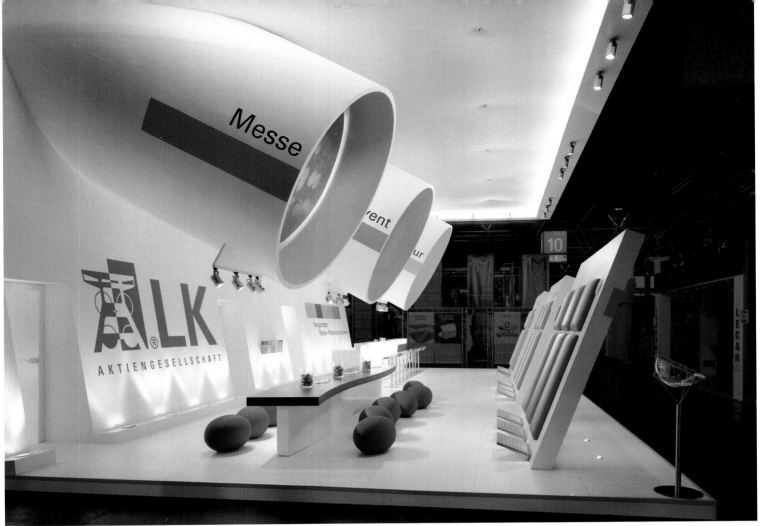

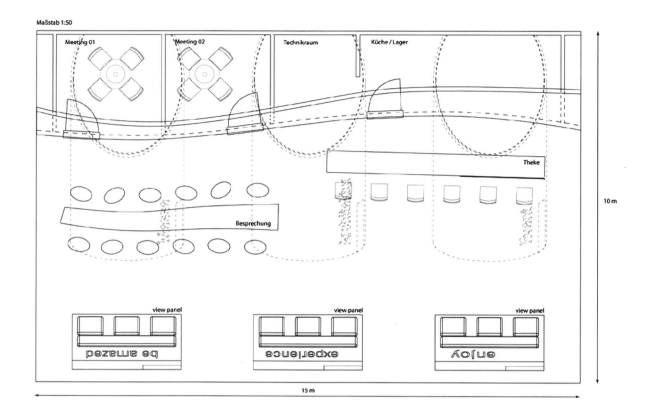

Maßstab 1:50

Meeting 01　　Meeting 02　　Technikraum　　Küche / Lager

10 m

Theke

Besprechung

view panel

be amazed

view panel

experience

view panel

enjoy

15 m

Think Kubik

Nike Football Park 2002

13 parks in 13 countries in 4 continents: Nike's vision was to celebrate soccer – the athletes and the fans – by building awesome, interactive Sports Parks. To move away from "mainstream" marketing they felt they could establish loyalty and respect with their youth target market by creating a raw, "street", underground feel.

Nike wanted their involvement with soccer to go beyond technical merit, into the importance of being a team. The significance of their Scorpion logo lies in the message "Every touch counts"; it's not important how fast you run, but that each movement contributes to your team's goal. This vision would tie into Nike's Legacy plan – to keep their marketing message alive by leaving something behind.

Nike hoped to reach 1.2 million kids during the 30-day period.

Exhibits International worked closely with Nike on the entire image, from the cage used in the television commercial, to helping Nike choose the most appropriate sites. They created incredible parks out of an abandoned abattoir, an unfinished subway line and an old ship to recreate parts of the television commercial.

Each Park contained indoor and outdoor interactive areas. The edge Nike desired was created through aged metal walls, cages around the interactive games areas, stacked oil drums and sea containers, spray painted logos and team posters plastering the walls. Each indoor venue housed the infamous "Scorpion Cage" that mirrored the television commercials and held the intense 3-minute final team matches. A central cage with a DJ added a "rave" feeling in the indoor section of each Park while video presentations and an animated scorpion played across large monitors.

The team of designers, technicians, builders and installers worked in 10 languages. The latest lighting and sound technology was used. Possibly the most logistically challenging project undertaken by EI, all 13 Parks launched on schedule and were a resounding success, exceeding Nike's attendance objective by thrilling 1.8 million kids.

Some countries have kept the Parks open as sports parks for public use. As many of these parks were built in run down areas, they are a satisfying contribution to Nike's legacy program.

CLIENT:
Nike, Inc.
LOCATION:
different countries
ARCHITECTURE:
Think Kubik
PHOTOGRAPHS:
Contributed by Think Kubik

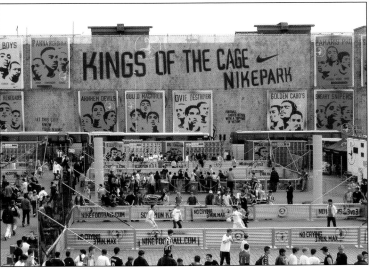

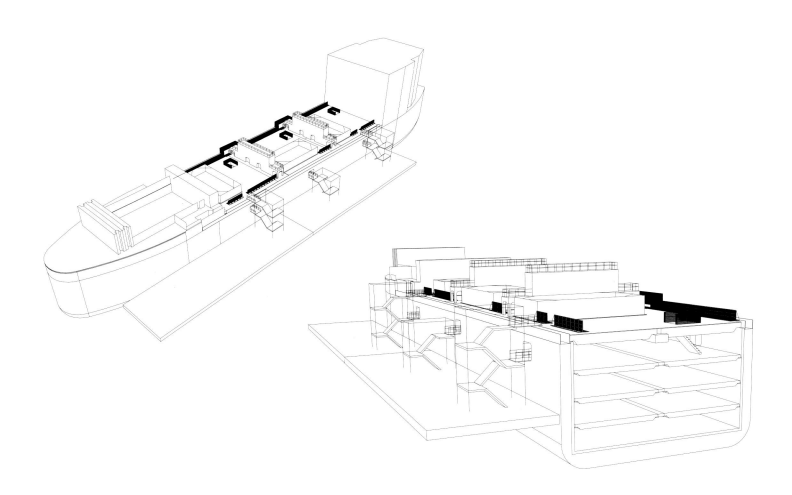

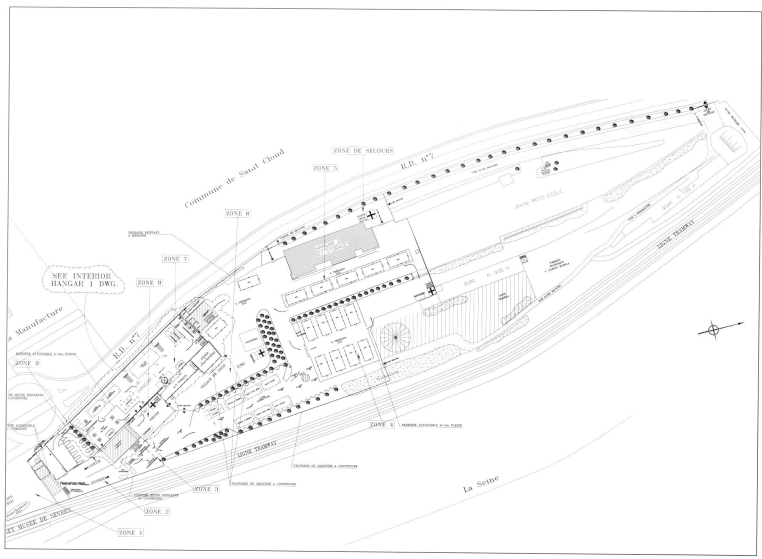

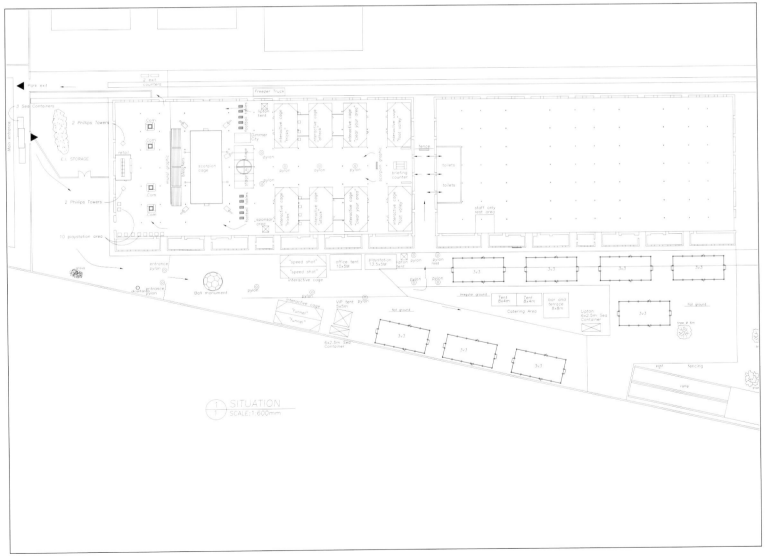

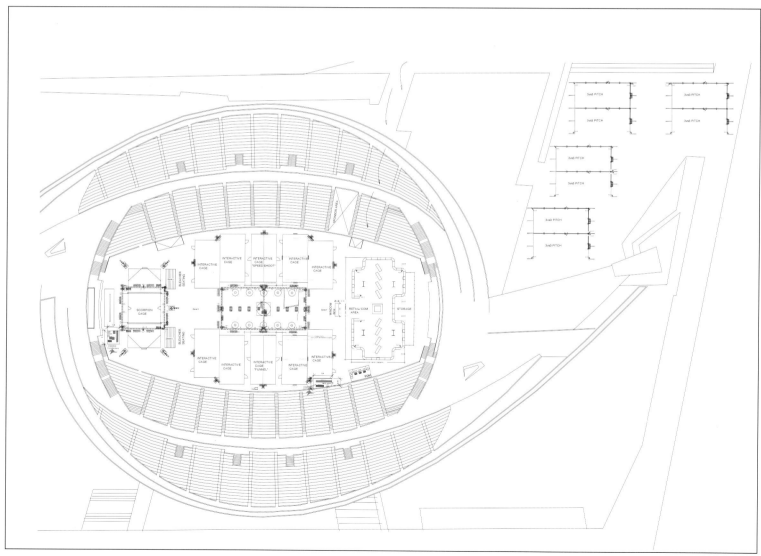

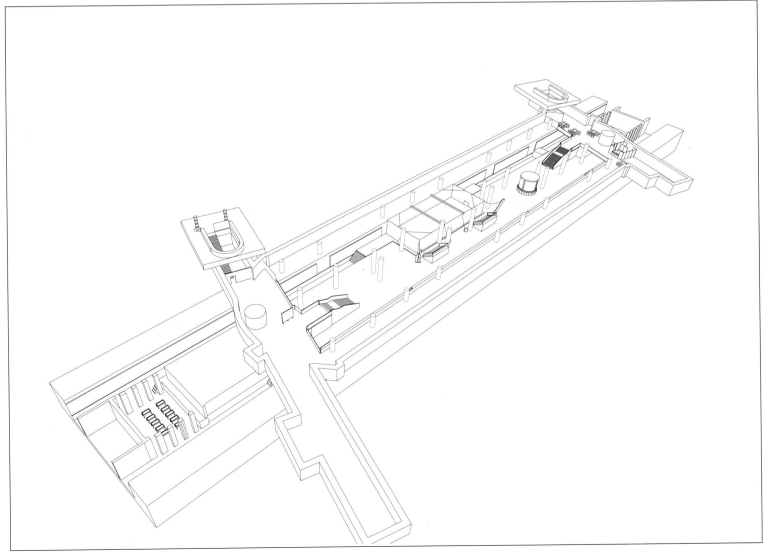

PTW Architects

Australian Pavilion

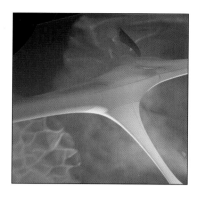

The Pavilion captures the interior atmosphere of the National Swimming Centre for the Beijing 2008 Olympics - 'Watercube' designed by PTW Architects, CSCEC+design and ARUP.

The Watercube's exterior relates to traditional Chinese architecture, an orthogonal counterpoint to the main Olympic stadium's curves, but the interior translates water and bubbles into fluidity and randomness.

Based on the existing 590' by 590' bubblebox, the lightweight construction of the new pavilion follows the tension lines of soap films, stretching between ground and sky. Since the early seventies and Frei Otto's soap bubble experiments with the Munich Olympic stadium, naturally evolving systems have gained ground in the field of new building typologies. Not exactly "designed", the pavilion is the most efficient subdivision of three-dimensional space, achieved with a flexible material that follows the forces of gravity, tension and growth, like a spider's web or a coral reef. Atmospheric animations projected onto it bring the pavilion to life as a surreal underwater experience.

The material is a fire rated Nylon Lycra Fabric. The installed object occupies a space of 79' x 33' x 20'. Packed for transport, it fits into a 1.64' x 1.64' x 2.30' sports bag and weighs 77 pounds. Assembly can be carried out in 1 hour, besides the rigging structure from which it is suspended. It was designed in 4 weeks, from the initial sketch to installation. PTW delivered a 3d computer-model, which Taiyo Membrane Corporation processed with a sailmaking software application to simulate stresses and tensions in the fabric, showing how the shape of membrane would respond. When the buildable design was ready, the 103 pieces of Lycra were stitched together in 200 hours of manual labour. The finished item was packed and transported to Beijing as "hand-luggage". Installed for the first time at the Stadia China exhibition within the budgeted sum, it has since travelled to DESIGNEX in Melbourne and to Dubai.

The project tests a new style of digital workflow, capable of generating a product of any shape out of lightweight material in an extremely short time. Easy to travel with, it can be built in 1 hour, and is fully reusable after the event.

LOCATION:
Stadia China, Beijing, China
ARCHITECTS:
PTW Architects
PHOTOGRAPHS:
Contributed by PTV

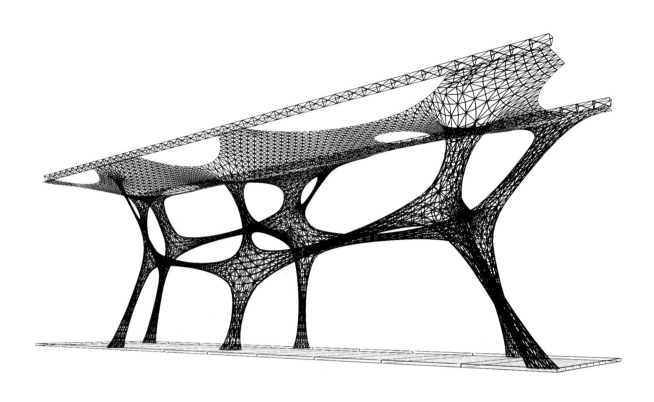

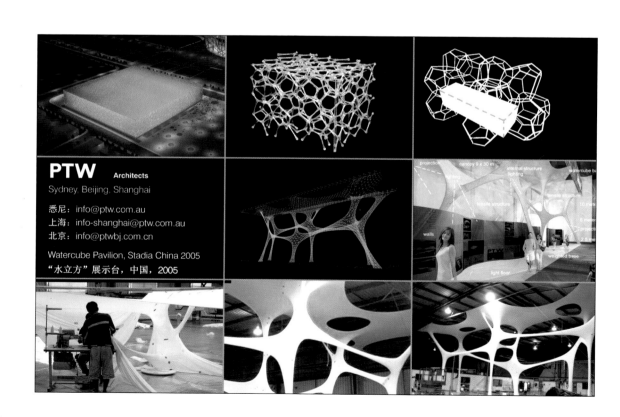

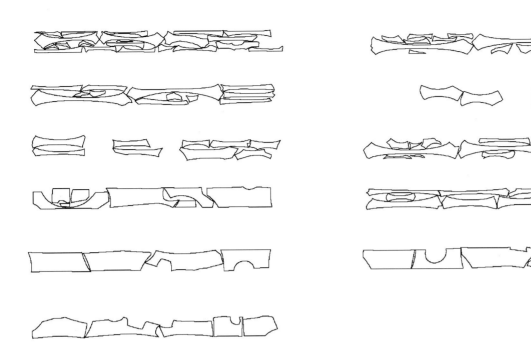

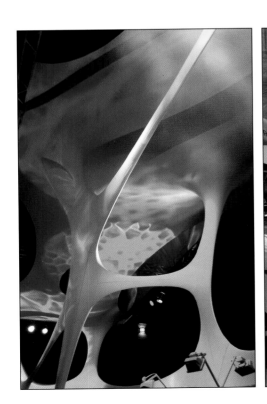

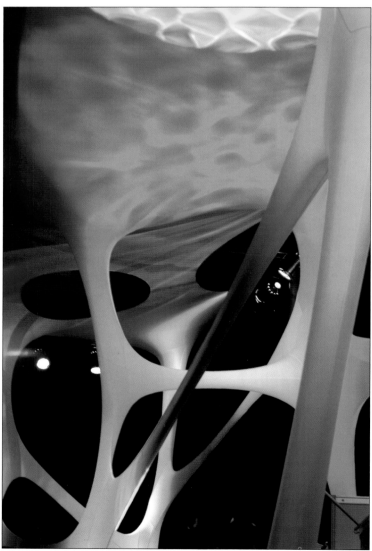

Quinze & Milan

Quinze & Milan

During this seventeenth yearly occasion in which Passagen offers a platform for the latest trends in modern design and lifestyle, there were over 150 shows and displays by international designers, installed all over the city, making Cologne into the Mecca of design. Galleries, shops, design studios, museums, and many other less likely venues attracted design fans to their door.

On the right hand riverbank of the Rhine, a new venue has opened under the name Design Post Köln. It is housed in a listed heritage building that used to belong to the Postal Service. Within the three wings of the former package post distribution halls, this exciting exhibition space contains a total of 20 display spaces, used throughout the whole year by top design firms and producers of international reputation. These permanent shows are aimed at the professionals in the field but also to private purchasers. The Design Post Köln adds a permanent magnet to the items that make Cologne a significant capital of this industry

The permanent showroom of Quinze & Milan, located in the Design Post building, has a total surface of about 200 sq meters. This year, in the context of the Cologne Design Week, the firm has created the magnum opus of their famous wooden structures. Having created such a sensation at various of the design shows they have attended, the relative permanence of their present venue has encouraged them to take the idea further, exploring the limit of its possibilities and creating a unique backdrop for the furniture and artifacts for which they are well-known. The gigantic installation interacts dramatically with the heroic functionality of the old steel and corrugated sheet structure in which it is housed. In total, the construction required 10 kilometers of wood, 50.000 nails, and 18 polyester cages. 5 members of the Quinze & Milan contractors work team constructed it from scratch in 5 days. The result not only makes a perfect setting for the company's display, but also advertises their capacity for truly challenging installations. The graphics are by the Glossy, Quinze & Milan's graphic section.

DESIGN & CLIENT:
Quinze & Milano
LOCATION:
Design Week 2006, Cologne, Germany
PHOTOGRAPHS:
Contributed by Quinze & Milan

Michael Young

Rambler

Born in the north of England in 1966, for the last five years Michael young has been based in Reykjavik, Iceland. From their secluded Nordic base, he and his wife, Katrin Petursdottir, add their grains of sand to the international projects in which they are involved.

The program of this trade show stand set out to unify about twenty different spaces, each with its corresponding function, within a total display area of 2000 sqm. An important part of the challenge was to find a way of linking these divergent functions, and illustrate Michael Young's strategies as a designer.

The program included an area for the press, several kiosks from which to sell the client's magazine, a coffee bar, a play area for the children to enjoy the stand, and an entertainment area for the adults to relax while the children were playing. A recycling system also had to be integrated in the show. The designers say they are pleased with the result, having created a space of relaxation in the context of a trade show stand.

A prominent magnet of the stand was a 1963 airstream mobile home, which had been completely gutted of its interior fixtures, and totally redesigned and fitted out by Michael Young, as a commission by Vooruitzicht, a projects developer from Belgium.

The stand was provided with a central meeting area to connect all the other spaces; this was called the Rambla. In the Young and Beautiful Café, all the wrappers, packaging and bottles were given the Young and Beautiful look, down to the last detail, including the Coca-Cola cans.

Three viewing boxes display a retrospective of Young's work, together with that of the British artist John Isaacs, his alter ego. One of the boxes is a tribute to the installation created by Verner Panton for the Interieur show in 1974, when he was the Guest of Honor.

According to Michael Young, this trade show is one of the few where design quality is seriously taken into consideration. He says that beyond fantasy, a good design consists of the perfect blend of many elements. It is the eloquent equilibrium between form, function and fantasy that has to be achieved, but they should not be considered autonomous items. The ingredient that must finally contain the rest is reality. Fantasy alone is absurd, it has to be made to be real. The designer claims that living in Iceland has allowed him a thinking space he needed, plus an interaction with open-minded manufacturers that have allowed him to ground his fantasy in the world of production and commerce.

CLIENT:
INTERIEUR02
LOCATION:
Interieur 2002, Kortrijk, Belgium
DATE OF PRODUCTION: 2002
DESIGNER:
Michael Young
ILLUSTRATOR:
Katrin Petursdottir
PHOTOGRAPHS:
Contributed by Michael Young Studio

 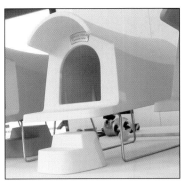  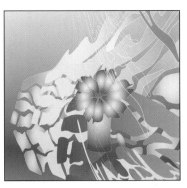